More Than
A
Pretty
Face

Authored by Christina Mead

Designed by Casey Olson

Copy editing by Elizabeth Bayardi, Amanda Grubbs, Joel Stepanek

Printed in the United States of America. Printed on acid-free paper.

This book is dedicated to my
goddaughter Mary.

I pray that you will always know how
beautiful you are, and that you are
loved and cherished
beyond measure.

CONTENT

Beginning with Beautiful............................pg. 7

If Only I was Pretty...................................pg. 13

If Only I was Thinner................................pg. 21

If Only I was Dating.................................pg. 29

If Only I was Famous................................pg. 37

More Than Pretty....................................pg. 43

Start with Love......................................pg. 53

People Need People.................................pg. 67

Child, Be Brave and Simple......................pg. 79

Reality Stars and Radical Honesty.........pg. 93

Royals in the Kingdom............................pg. 107

Givers Will Receive.................................pg. 117

A Beautiful Imperfection......................pg. 133

BEGINNING WITH BEAUTIFUL

"I think I might be the wrong person to write this book."

That thought won't leave me. But I also can't shake the feeling deep in my soul that I have to... that I must... that it's necessary that I write this book.

I've taken it to God in prayer so many times and every single time I've asked Him to please let me off the hook for this one.

He hasn't.

Maybe it's because I need this book more than anyone else. If I'm being honest with myself and with you, this is still my number one struggle – to see myself as beautiful. It's something I've wrestled with my whole life.

There have been many ups and downs in this struggle, but the one thing that remains with me always, like a tiny voice in the back of my head, is the message that God's way is different. His way is better. He has wisdom about beauty, encouragement for the bad days, and a message of hope for our broken hearts. All of these things the saints have discovered and lived out in incredible ways. Their lives are an example to me of how to be a woman of God, and live assured of my beauty no matter what is going on around me. I want to share that with you.

Also, I know that the truth about beauty can be found in God's word, Holy Scripture. Many, many days those words of my Creator, my Savior, my King, those are the only words that can comfort me. Those are the words that are the light of truth illuminating my wounds and healing my brokenness. I want to share those words with you too.

Lastly, the mind is a powerful weapon – for good or bad. I've spent many years learning to understand the power of my thoughts, and how to harness that power for good. It's a huge mistake to think that God only wants us to get on our knees and pray in order to get through the bumps in the road of this life. He gave us our mind, our intellect, and our will in order that we might learn from the sciences and be transformed by the renewal of our minds (Romans 12:2). There's so much in this regard that has helped me begin to see myself as beautiful. I want to share that with you too.

But don't get me wrong; I'm not saying I've figured this out perfectly. Far from it. Remember? Begging

God that He ask someone else to write this book – that was me.

Yet here I am. Putting words down, sharing my heart – all the good and bad – despite the thought it shouldn't be me. Because, my dear sister, if I waited until I had it figured out, until every day I woke up and walked through my day feeling like the most beautiful woman in the world, I don't think this would ever get written.

And I know it needs to be done.

I know there are girls everywhere who struggle with feeling like they aren't beautiful. I see you. I see you pulling at your clothes, making sure you hide all the right things, and highlight the other things. I see you adjusting your body in your seat, constantly monitoring how you appear to others. I see you taking pictures with your face and arm and hip at the right angles for optimal attractiveness.

I see you exhausted by it all.

I see you tired of the feeling that it's never enough; that at the end of the day you'll never be beautiful.

I see you because I am you. I'm right there beside you feeling the same things, fighting the same demons. We're in this together.

And if we're in this together, then I have to write this book for you... for us. Any little bit of wisdom I've gained from this fight I want to pass on to you, even if it just helps a little. I have to add some good, some light of truth to this conversation because we are bombarded on all sides by voices telling us lies about beauty. I'm tired of it, and I'm tired of seeing you fight it alone.

We deserve better. We deserve more.

I am better than the lies the world tells me. I am more than my brokenness. I am more than the negative thoughts I hear in my head, than the mean things I tell myself. I am more than this culture's definition of beauty. I am better than the desire to be a Photo-shopped model. I am more than a pretty face.

My hope and my prayer for you is that you'll be able to see yourself as more too. I want you to look in the mirror and know you are beautiful. Because you are.

This book is a story about me.

It's the only story I can tell with the raw, honest vulnerability this topic deserves. It's a story of what I've been through inside my heart and mind as I process the world around me and what I see when I look in the mirror.

It's a sad story in some places, but a really great story in other places. It's full of ups and downs, like all of our lives are.

This story is about my relationship with my body, with my thoughts, with my heart, and above all, about my relationship with God. He hasn't given up on me. On the days I've hated myself the most, He's loved me the most. When I was stuck in negative self-talk, He is the one who whispered encouragement to me through His words in the Bible, through nature, through other people, and through grace. I believe it was His guiding hand that led me to learn about some female saints who would be key in helping me understand how to finally see myself as beautiful, and believe it in the depths of my soul.

I want to share all of this with you. I want you to know you're not alone. I want you to know the ways that I've tried and failed to feel pretty and how I ultimately learned to see my inner beauty. I failed a bunch of times before I found strategies that work, but I want to tell you about it all – the good and the bad. I want you to be able to understand what doesn't work, so that you can throw it out and focus on what does work.

Honestly, I don't remember when I started believing that I wasn't beautiful. When I try to think about it, it seems like I've struggled with it for my whole life.

IF ONLY I WAS PRETTY

When I was little, I took ballet classes. I remember always feeling chubby and uncomfortable in my dance costumes. They were supposed to be tight, but I had a heightened sense of how the tight lines made other parts of my body bulge. Was it supposed to be that way? I looked around and saw that not everyone's bodies looked like that. Something was wrong with me then I concluded. I was the different one. I continued taking dance classes for a couple years, but I never wanted to take tap dance because I was afraid everyone would only look at my flabby bits bouncing up and down with each peppy step.

For church on Sunday, I would always wear my coat all through Mass because I didn't like how I looked in my dresses.

I snuck food when I was hungry because I was afraid someone would see me and question why I was eating, maybe even judge me for my food choices. I learned exactly how to lift and replace the lid of the cookie jar without making a sound.

I remember being a pre-teen and going sledding in the winter with my sisters. One time I made a comment about how if me and my sister both got on the sled it would go really fast because I was so heavy. She told me I was wrong, that I wasn't that heavy. I told her exactly how much I weighed, saying I know that's probably more than her. She agreed. I did weigh more than her. The sled did go really fast. I felt pretty low.

I remember watching TV and movies and comparing every inch of myself to the young actresses I idolized. They always gave this message that everyone was important, everyone was good — but at the same time they looked perfect. And I did not. I scrutinized my frizzy hair down to my oversized middle school feet and I began to loathe myself and wonder how I could change.

I started dieting before I was even in high school. I remember exactly which fad diets were the craze of the year and I jumped on board as best as I could, restricting my food in ways that wouldn't be too noticeable to the rest of my family. I didn't want them to question me. I didn't want them to know I felt so badly about myself, and that some days I even hated myself.

Almost constantly I told myself that I wasn't good enough. I wasn't pretty. The feelings that accompanied those thoughts left me hopeless. I would roll my eyes every time I heard those words "You're a beautiful daughter of God!" What does that even mean? Because it sure didn't feel like it applied to me.

And what could I ever do?

I wanted to blame God.

Sometimes I did.

If He is really all-powerful, I thought, *He didn't have to make me this way. He could have given me a different body, different influences, different messages.*

I couldn't understand how I was supposed to see myself as "beautifully and wonderfully made." I felt like there was a mistake when it came to me. I felt like I was never beautiful, like I never will be beautiful, like there's nothing I can do.

I know you might feel like that too sometimes. I know there have been times in your life when you were growing up that convinced you you're not beautiful. Maybe someone told you to your face. Maybe it was implied. Maybe you just tell yourself so often that you've forgotten when it started. I get it.

I know what it feels like to get dressed in the morning and look in the mirror, hoping one more time to like what you see... only to find out once again that your heart falls in despair. You still hate what you see.

"I look so fat in this."

"Why did I ever buy this shirt? It looks horrible."

"My thighs are so gross."

"No amount of makeup will ever improve this face."

"I hate myself."

"I can't go out like this."

"No one will ever love me."

"Why did God make me this way?"

The list of insults could go on and on. Do you hear these words in your own voice? Do you see your fallen, sad face saying these things? Do you feel that pit in your stomach because you know all too well the depths of self-loathing you can reach?

Do you feel that spark of hope that we have something in common because I know what it feels like too? Do you know that a lot of women feel this way and now is the time to start talking about it, to bring it into the light? Do you know that God has something better in store for us? That He doesn't want you to keep feeling this way?

Do you know there are very, very real and practical things you can do to change the story of self-hate in your life? Do you know it's in your power to rewrite the script of negativity that's on repeat in your head?

Are you tired of it? Do you want something different?

The world doesn't want us to break this cycle because money is made off of our low self-esteem and our search for what will make us pretty. Every ad you see for a health or beauty product is being sold to you on the premise that you need something else to feel beautiful... so buy their stuff. Spend your money on one more tube of lipstick because it's finally going to be the right one.

When we women are secure in who we are, we aren't constantly searching for the next best thing to make us better... and then companies lose out on more money. They don't want to lose money so they want us to keep feeling insufficient. Companies want you to feel like you're never good enough. Isn't that sad?

And then let's talk about the entertainment industry. Movies, TV shows, and music videos often portray women as "things" for the pleasure of others. Women are seen as accessories added to the story for the appeal they add visually to the audience.

Girls are given the message from the moment they start consuming media that they aren't good enough. The idea of perfection that they see portrayed is not only unachievable, it is unreal. It isn't grounded in reality because it's either faked through Photoshop, or unattainable because of the unrealistic amount of time and money that a model or celebrity has to spend on their outward appearance.

And yet, I still looked to all the beautiful women I saw on TV and in movies and magazines. They were the standard I compared myself to. I'm a fan of reading too and it's funny because even though it's not a visual media, whenever I read about a girl whom I admired, in my mind she looked perfect too. The book could literally say, "she was pale with frizzy hair" and in my mind I'd be like, *yeah but she probably had a perfect hourglass figure (unlike ME) and no acne on her pale skin (unlike ME) and all the boys don't even notice her frizzy hair because she's a beautiful blond (unlike ME).* I was relentless in tearing myself down and calling out my imperfections. It was exhausting.

I wanted something more for myself and I know you sure as heck do too. I got really tired of feeling like I wasn't beautiful, and then feeling confused because I knew God wanted me to know I was beautiful. I felt so stuck. It was like I was stuck in the middle of a game of tug-of-war. I'm standing in the middle just trying to stay upright, trying to remain balanced. On one end I have this little devil insisting I'm not beautiful and never will be. At the other end I have an angel telling me that God made me beautiful. I get pulled both directions. I keep looking back and forth, not sure who to believe. I can't keep a steady footing in life because I'm constantly getting yanked either way. I didn't know what to trust, or how to accurately measure how pretty I was. This led me to look to the scale and the scale alone.

IF ONLY I WAS THINNER

I started measuring my worth by the number on the scale when I was in middle school. Over time that number didn't just represent what growth percentile I was in, it became a measure of how close to or far away I was from the standard of perfection I had set for myself.

My mind can be brutally, relentlessly mean to myself. Not to other people though! I am gentle down to the bone with other people. If I pass someone on the street and they have no makeup, they're overweight, their hair is in a top knot, but not like a "cute" top knot... my mind is like, *oh my gosh that sweet person is so beautiful rocking the natural, no makeup look and I bet they've had a long day and I just want to hug them and tell them they are loved! And they look so soft to hug, I wish I was their friend.*

And then they walk by me with an odd look on their face because I was staring at them with a little, longing smile that they had no idea meant, "can I be your friend and tell you you're loved" instead of "I'm crazy and smiling awkwardly to hide it."

But when it comes to me...

Whole.

Other.

Story.

I will berate myself all day for the two donuts I ate. Last week.

I will allow the number on the scale to dictate if I have a good day or a bad day.

I won't go to a friend's birthday party if I "feel fat" that day and can't find something to wear.

I refuse to go rock climbing because I'm afraid of how the required body harness will make my butt look.

I have cried in dressing rooms in the mall.

I have laid in bed not wanting to get up and face another day because it meant facing myself in the mirror one more time.

I have been out on a date and not finished my food, even though I wanted to, because I'm afraid of what the guy will think.

For so long I have thought that if only I was thinner, then I would finally be pretty! I would feel great about myself. I would love my body. I would be more confident because I wouldn't be worried about how I look or what I'm eating. I would be happy more often.

The quest for "thinness" took me down the path of every kind of diet you can think of. No carbs, no sugar, no fats, no gluten, no animal products, no fun, no smiles, no good cheer. I've done it all, including, but not limited to: lots of running, swimming, lifting, cycling, walking, yoga, and sprints to and from the kitchen to grab more chocolate chips.

So why was nothing working? I was caught in a cycle of restricting myself so harshly, losing a couple of pounds, being excited about that and wanting to celebrate, but also exhausted from the restrictions... so then I would binge and have a whole carton of ice cream and bag of chocolate chips and totally wreck my metabolism under the banner of "I deserve it."

Cue the self-hatred again.

It was an unending dieting-merry-go-round with no pretty ponies and only weight machines to sit on.

Until one spring, I decided to do things a little differently. I was struggling with stress and anxiety at the time and my therapist recommended I go "back to the basics of self-care," as she says, to make sure that every week I prioritized three things: prayer, spending time with friends, and exercise.

So I hung up a calendar in my kitchen for visual accountability and I would write on the days what I had done to exercise. Some days said "20 minute run" or "30 minute walk" or "18 mile bike ride" and then some days were blank. I made it a challenge to work out more days each month.

Not only was I feeling energized and stronger, I was also feeling a lot less stressed. I woke up happier and more refreshed. Overall, I just felt awesome! I wasn't training for anything. I wasn't trying to reach any workout goal except "workout more days." I didn't shame myself for missed days, I just made sure to have something on the calendar the next day, even if it was just a 15 minute walk. Anything is better than being on the couch, I told myself.

Over the course of a couple months, I also started making smarter choices in what I ate. Read as: less chocolate chips, more broccoli. One day I got on the scale and saw that I had lost about 20 lbs.

I couldn't believe it. Here I was! I was thinner than I had been in years! I remember going for a bike ride that day and I had some tears flowing down my cheeks. No drivers, that's not rain, it's coming from my eyes. I was grateful, I was excited, I was euphoric! Twenty pounds less of me! What did it mean for my life?!

I thought it meant that I would finally, once and for all, see myself as beautiful. I thought it meant I would wake up and go to bed knowing that I was beautiful. I would have a new experience of life - the new, improved, *beautiful* Christina Mead.

The feelings lasted for *maybe* 36 hours... and I was asleep for 9 of them.

It turned out losing weight changed nothing. I could not have been more devastated when I realized that despite being 20 pounds lighter, I still criticized every bit of myself. I still saw the flaws! I saw that even though my shorts fit better, there was still cellulite on the back of my thighs... and I hated it. Even though I put on a smaller dress size for a date, I still lacked some confidence. I still pulled at it every five minutes to make sure it was sitting just right on me.

Even though I looked a little better in my selfies, and sometimes thought, *yeah I look gooooood*. I still felt that I was left out of the "beautiful club" somehow. It wasn't enough. There was more weight to lose. There was more makeup to wear. There were better, more expensive clothes to buy. I still wasn't good enough.

Not to mention within a year I regained the weight. My temporary, euphoric day and a half stint in the land of the beautiful-thinner-population didn't change me for the better.

One day I called my friend as I was hysterically crying, sitting in my car outside my doctor's office. "All she talked about was my weight," I whined, between gasps for breath in the effort it took to cry and talk at the same time.

I had gone to the doctor to talk about something 100% different than my weight, but it was what she had focused on. I felt so defeated. Yes, I had gained some weight. Yes, I wasn't within my ideal range. Yes, I knew I overate during the holidays.

I was crushed. In my mind, the doctor's concern over the number on the scale (and after a sizeable breakfast at that!) was an attack on me and my worth. It destroyed me. I had done the best I could to not cry in front of the doctor and as soon as I walked out and the door shut behind me, the waterworks began. I stood at the railing outside her second floor office and allowed myself to have a moment of grief fueled by self-loathing. No people walking below, that's not rain, it's coming from my eyes.

Losing. Gaining. Bingeing. Restricting. Pinching. Pulling. Scrutinizing. Sweating.

Nothing left a lasting change on how I felt about myself. In the end, the years of getting on and off the scale only left me exhausted. I did not feel more beautiful. The one thing I was hoping would change everything in my life — losing weight — did nothing but leave me more raw than I started as.

I realized that I was focused on losing weight because I actually hated myself. When I finally lost a sizeable amount, I became more harsh with my self criticism. When I gained it back, I also gained a renewed hatred and sensitivity about my size so that when the professional I pay to give me advice on my health dared to make a comment about it — I was destroyed.

Looking back I can point a finger at everything and say, "What an unhealthy way to live and think!" But in that moment, in those years... I was suffering. And it was very real. I didn't see any way out and I couldn't think of it getting better. If being thinner wasn't the answer to feeling more beautiful — what was? My whole life I had believed that one thing and when that one thing was proven wrong I felt like the floor had crumbled beneath me.

There had to be something else.

IF ONLY
I WAS
DATING

"What about this mole right here?" I asked him.

Not giving him time to answer, I asked, "What about how sometimes I have a double chin in photos?"

"What about my arms? They're too big, right?" I insisted as I kept pressing him with questions.

"And what about these love handles?" I asked as I grabbed onto my sides and squeezed what was there, accentuating on purpose the extra pounds I knew I had around my lower waist. If he said he hated them, I would be destroyed. If he said he didn't mind, I would be bewildered and doubtful.

He couldn't really win.

"I also have this single, embarrassing, thick black hair that grows out of one spot on the center of my chin... what do you think about that?"

Oh my gosh I just asked that. I had shocked even myself.

I looked down, not even wanting to make eye contact with him, this guy I had been dating. I couldn't believe I brought up the chin hair. What was I thinking? If there's anything that should remain a secret for my entire life, a secret so severe that I take it to my grave never revealing it to another soul... it's the chin hair, Christina. Come on. It's like you have one-thousandth of a beard and that's so gross! And even though I check for it religiously and always pluck that stubborn thing as soon as it has the boldness to rear it's big, thick head... it should never be mentioned. It is "the-thing-that-must-not-be-named" that resides on my face.

But here I was, caught up in the whirlwind of feelings that come along with falling in love, and I was already making rash decisions! I was bringing up all the things I hated about myself and pointing out my flaws — including the thick black chin hair. Shouldn't I be hiding my flaws instead of parading them under a spotlight for him?

Maybe... but all I wanted was to have a man tell me it was all okay. I wanted him to tell me I was beautiful despite those flaws. I wanted to know he could look past them and still love me.

Then at least when he put his arms around me and I heard the voice in my head telling me again that I should be smaller so his arms would wrap around me even more than they did... then I could silence that voice by remembering his answers to my litany of faults.

I always thought dating would annihilate those doubts about my own beauty. My reasoning was that if someone liked me enough to ask me out, that must mean I'm beautiful enough to be wanted, cherished, and loved. I thought dating would cure my insecurities. I thought it would change me and how I saw myself.

I saw other girls who looked so happy and confident in relationships. Those girls I saw walking through the mall holding the hand of a cute guy, laughing together, and taking selfies — surely they thought of themselves as beautiful because they had a man right there affirming it!

I wanted that. I had tried other things to make me feel beautiful and nothing so far had worked. I decided a boyfriend would fix it.

So I sought out the attention of guys. It took a little time at first. I thought I had to take the right selfies from the right angles. I had to learn the best ways to flirt. I had to master the art of the subtle arm touch. It worked. They were texting me. Calling me. Asking me to "hang" and "chill" and ever so rarely go on a real, official "date." I even kissed some of them, because I thought that was one more level of approval that would affirm that I was wanted, desireable... beautiful.

And yet, it wasn't working. Late at night, alone with my thoughts, my ideas about my self-worth did not improve... they only got worse.

As I was looking to the opposite gender to affirm my worth and beauty, I was only falling deeper into the hole of self-loathing. Instead of feeling more confident, I was relying more on attention. Instead of feeling more empowered, I felt powerless. Every break up was another chance for me to blame myself for not being good enough, even if I was the one doing the breaking up! In those cases, I blamed myself for making a poor dating choice. Everything was my fault.

Not to mention I kept feeling used. In my quest to feel pretty, I wrongfully allowed myself to be with guys who only really wanted me there because I was a warm body. I was an object; a body prop. I was a fixture in their lives. They didn't appreciate me for me, they appreciated me because I provided status. Having me meant they had a "girlfriend" or a "date" for that weekend wedding. Their beloved Aunt Margie could be proud of them for once. They didn't care that I was intelligent, or kind, or talented... they only cared that I was a girl and I was single and ready to mingle.

I didn't feel more beautiful. I felt small and cheap.

I remember one time I was a couple weeks into dating a guy and things were going great. We would have such a fun time together — lots of laughter and inside jokes. Lots of listening to great music and watching movies and eating take-out because why not wreak havoc on our 20-something-year-old bodies while we're young and free? We loved going for drives in his truck, not even going anywhere in particular, but just chatting about our days, about life, about God and religion. Sometimes at a red light or a crossroads I would call out "Left!" or "Right!" and he'd yank the wheel accordingly and we'd see where we would end up (and what take-out food we could acquire while there).

It was going well except that I was uneasy about one thing: he never told anyone about me. He was really close with his mom, but every time I asked if he had told her yet that we were dating, he said no.

He lived with a ridiculous number of roommates, like five or something (and a dog) and I never met any of them, despite the fact that we hung out at his house pretty often. He would somehow manage to only have me over when they weren't around, or we would go to parts of the house where no one else was.

There was one time we saw one of his roommates, and he stopped to talk to him. I was literally standing right there and I was not introduced to the roommate, nor acknowledged by said roommate.

I was actually just a temporary fixture in his life. I was there to solve his current problem — boredom. And I was doing a great job. There was no need to incorporate me into his whole life because I was only there for a brief time, and my only purpose was to temporarily suppress his loneliness. While at the same time, I was committing the same injustice. I was using him to fill a void in my life. I wanted him to fix my insecurity. I wanted him to make me feel pretty.

I felt small and cheap. Not dignified and worth a great deal, or a great love. I was just a girl to fill an empty space in his life. That didn't make me feel good. I didn't feel beautiful at all. And that's what I thought dating would do for me! I thought it would help me feel beautiful. Well it wasn't. Dating didn't change anything. It didn't fix my problems. It didn't change the voices in my head. It only exaggerated them.

I realized it's easier to give power to the negativity in your mind when you have a compassionate someone next to you who is willing to listen to you. Have you ever noticed that? If you have things to get done, and places to be, and people to care for, you're less likely to give headspace to the negative thoughts and mean self-accusations swirling in your head.

But give me a man by my side who has all evening to sit and listen to my complaints and I just let that self-hate run wild. I don't have to learn to speak truth to myself when I can bottle up all that self-hate and spill it out on someone else who cares for me. They can counter it for me. They can comfort me. They can tell me I'm beautiful. They can hold me while I cry. They can make me tea and keep asking if I'm okay. They can give me the attention and distraction to hold everything else at bay.

So that's where I was that day when I was grilling my boyfriend about my list of flaws, naming specific things I hated about myself so he could tell me I'm perfect and calm the monster in my mind.

I waited breathlessly for his response.

And now it doesn't even matter what he said. If he spoke sweet words of encouragement to me, naming all the ways I was perfect in his eyes... it didn't matter. Deep down, I still didn't feel pretty and the cycle would repeat itself with my next boyfriend. Dating didn't fix how I saw myself. No matter who thinks you're beautiful, and affirms that in their words, actions, and declaration of dating status on social media... none of it will make a difference if you don't learn to see your own beauty.

I learned that lesson the hard way as time and again I asked someone else to fix what was broken inside myself. Those guys didn't know my whole story. All they could do was say the same things that the guy before them had said.

No matter how many times I heard the words, "you're so beautiful" from the mouth of a man, it changed nothing deep in my heart.

IF ONLY I WAS FAMOUS

When I realized dating may not be the answer, I decided that maybe I would believe I was pretty if I could be affirmed by lots and lots of people — maybe that would help. Having one boyfriend at a time affirm me wasn't enough, and I've had enough of my mom telling me I'm pretty. I needed more people! Moms are like required to say that anyway, aren't they? I came from her womb, I am flesh of her flesh! She signed the mom contract that all moms sign in the hospital. Have you heard of it? Before they discharge new moms from the hospital they have to sign a contract (with the blood from the umbilical cord) that says they will always tell their child they're perfect, always dress them in the most uncomfortable church clothes for holidays, always make them eat their vegetables, and always give them an embarrassing haircut around about the age of five. It's a very official document.

No, but really. I felt like if only I had the praise of more people that it would validate me and my worth. If more people liked me in person, and clicked "like" on my social media posts, then that meant I was valued, didn't it?

It wasn't about who I was deep inside. They didn't need to see that (and I was certain they wouldn't want to!).

Initially, when I joined the world of social media, I only presented the best version of myself to the world. Let's all be honest here — everyone knows what it's like to take 75 selfies all at *slightly* different angles and then post the one that was most flattering for your jawline and cheekbones. I am totally guilty of doing that. How I looked dictated whether I would post something, or whether I even felt good about myself that day.

I would also, on occasion, do things simply because I knew it would make a good post on social media and was likely to get me a lot of likes — therefore making me feel good about myself. I sought out unique people, places, and experiences, all while wearing different never-before-seen-on-Instagram outfits, not because I sincerely wanted to have those experiences, but because I thought it would get me more attention from my followers. Talk about authenticity. It was anything but authentic!

It was exhausting. I couldn't keep that up for very long at all.

However... it was working. I was getting more likes, more followers, more comments... and more self-esteem... or so I thought. It felt like self-esteem, even though it was built upon the weak foundation of social media and lasted only about as long as a popsicle in an Arizona summer.

Around the time I started to gain more attention on social media, I also started doing some work as a public speaker. The first time I got on a stage I was so scared my legs were shaking (and I realized it was a really bad time to wear heels). I remember in that moment being amazed that wobbling knees were actually a real thing and not just a figure of speech, or a thing in cartoons!

I had planned a great talk. I had practiced and practiced, making sure all my jokes were well-timed, and my facial expressions on point. I held that microphone like a pro, looked out at all the faces staring back at me... and freaked out. But I delivered my talk and at the end — applause. Slaps on the back of congratulations. Praise. Admiration. Validation of my well-timed jokes and on point facial expressions.

I thought to myself — *this is what it's like... this is what it's like to be popular, to be liked, to be pretty. I made it; I'm here.* I felt like I was on top of the world!

The next person walked up to me to shake my hand except she didn't tell me what a great job I did and how funny I was and how pretty I am in that adorable dress... nope. She told me all the things I had done wrong. She pointed out the things she didn't agree with and wanted to debate me about.

I was crushed.

At the core of my being I want to be a people pleaser and please all people (all the time). I just want everyone to be happy. That was not happening in this moment and for the second time within an hour my knees were wobbling.

My happy rug of fame was ripped out from underneath me and I fell on my butt, my pride knocked down a notch or eight.

This happened multiple times. I would get off stage after giving a talk and almost immediately hear what I had done wrong, either from a face in the crowd, or from the face in the mirror.

It turned out that no matter how loving the faces, how loud the applause, or how many people wanted to take selfies with me afterwards — it didn't last. The temporary surge of self-esteem from the admiration of crowds wasn't enough to transform years of negativity into unconditional self-love. Just as four million likes on one photo can't heal a broken heart. I'll never forget hearing about one reality TV star who had been told her lips were too small when she was a child. No matter how much fame she achieved on TV and online, it wasn't enough to make her believe she was beautiful and that her lips were fine as God made them. Millions of likes and comments couldn't change what she had decided in her mind and in her heart. Someone had mired her view of herself and that had hurt her.

Finally her broken heart led her to a doctor to "fix" what wasn't pretty enough on her.

Fame couldn't convince her she was beautiful.

Just as it couldn't convince me. I thought it would because I bought into the lie that our worth and our value must first be recognized and approved by other people in order for me to recognize and approve of my value and worth in myself. I believed I would find peace in knowing that I am pretty if I had the attention of the masses.

Instead, fame creates a pretty brutal spotlight. More followers means more people to critique you, and more people for whom I felt the need to appear "perfect."

I have more social media followers than I ever thought I would, my name is easy to Google, there are videos of me on YouTube, I've stood on stages, and I've had hundreds of blogs published... but none of that could convince me I was pretty. It didn't change what I saw in the mirror when I looked at myself. I still only saw my physical self. I was stuck looking at my body, only seeing skin deep.

Nothing could make me "feel" as pretty as I wanted, no matter how much weight I lost, or what high goal I pursued, or what man I was dating. The "pursuit of pretty" kept ending in failure, right back where I was as a child. I was convinced I never was and never will be pretty.

But praise God, that's not where the story ends.

MORE THAN PRETTY

One of the things I love to do is ride my bike. I know I mentioned this before when talking about trying to lose weight. I became slightly addicted to it as an adult when I realized it's still just as awesome as it was when I was a kid. As a kid, I used to ride my bike around the neighborhood with my siblings and friends for hours until the streetlights came on and we had to get home for bed.

Fifteen years later riding my bike, there were fewer curfews and more speeds; what's not to love? Plus, being alone on a bike covering miles and miles of sidewalk along a canal provides a perfect opportunity for some audio entertainment. I often listen to music, podcasts, or books while I'm riding. The best is when I'm at a really good part of the book and just randomly pump my fist in the air, or a random hilarious part and I let out an audible laugh... right at the same moment I'm passing someone.

I really have given up the hope that I'm "normal."

I'll never forget one ride I took while listening to a podcast from a Christian pastor from the Southeast about God and the Gospel message. The pastor was recounting a story that happened recently among his friends. His church was putting on a big conference for hundreds of thousands of people. In fact, there were *so* many people they couldn't even fit them all in one place. So the crowd was split between one "bigger" location, and one smaller, "off-site" location. The off-site location was going to have some of their own stuff going on, but for most of it they were going to be watching a live broadcast of the bigger space.

The whole event was going to start with two live worship bands playing music in the separate venues for the crowds. Beginning a big event, there's always a ton of energy and excitement from the participants. It's a perfect time to channel that excitement into praise of our Creator, God, and to unite in prayer to set the tone.

In planning this event, the leaders thought, *"How amazing would it be if during the opening session of praise and worship, in the middle of one of the songs they surprise the crowd with a Mega-Christian-Musician appearing on stage to lead them in song and in prayer?"*

But what about having two locations? How would that work? They didn't want the people in the smaller, off-site location to be all bummed out that they were missing the incredible surprise of the Mega-Christian-Musician!

"What's going to happen?!" I thought… or perhaps accidentally said out loud while whizzing down the canal sidewalk on my bike. *"Ignore me, I'm not normal!!"* I should be saying to everyone passing me by.

Back to the Mega-Christian-Conference with the Mega-Christian-Musician. Their master plan, though it would be challenging, was to have both live bands at both sites start out playing the song "Our God" at exactly the same time for the two crowds. And then (At the height! The Climax! The crescendo of the song!) the Mega-Christian-Musician would run out on the bigger stage and start singing a part of one of his own songs that would fit perfectly into the bridge of Our God! The off-site screen, instead of watching the other crowd praising, would suddenly see AND hear the musician on their live feed. There wouldn't even be a break in the music. It would be seamless. It would be incredible.

Everything was planned perfectly. The Mega-Christian-Musician secret was well-kept. None of the participants had any idea of what was going to happen. The organizers knew they were just going to *love* it. They would go *wild*.

As the pastor tells the story, he says that there were two production coordinators in each arena in charge of making sure everything was going according to plan for the Big-Surprise. The two worship leaders in each arena were going to be keeping the same time and the same beat using what's called a "click track" in their in-ear monitors — it's like a metronome in their ears.

It was time to start and both bands started singing:

"Water you turned into wine.... Opened the eyes of the blind... There's no one like you, none like you..."

Everything was going great in the big arena. But in the smaller arena, the sound producer was watching both the worship band in front of him, and the band in the larger arena to make sure they were in sync.

"Our God is greater... Our God is stronger... God you are higher than any other."

He watched one band play that part of the song, and saw those lyrics on the screen over at the big arena.

And then about 15 seconds later, the band in from of him sang the same part:

"Our God is greater... Our God is stronger... God you are higher than any other..."

Something had happened. The bands weren't at the same part of the song at the same time. Who had messed up? Who had sped up, who had slowed down? This wasn't supposed to happen. The worship leader in the smaller arena must *not* have had the click track going in his ear because he wasn't on the beat. The production coordinator panicked. He only had a minute before Mega-Christian-Musician was going to come out and interject the song with his own unique bridge. However, if the off-site location wasn't at the same break in the song, it wouldn't work right. They would still be singing the chorus and it would be really awkward. The hype wouldn't be the same.

The production coordinator had to make a really fast decision. He had the ability to speak directly into the earpiece of the worship leader in front of him in the small arena who was in the middle of singing the song. So because he's brilliant, he just started singing the part of the song that he wanted them to be on. He sang the words into the worship leaders in-ear monitor praying he would understand what he was attempting to communicate.

"Our God is greater... Our God is stronger..."

The worship leader, as he was playing an instrument, and singing, *also* listened to the producer singing different words in his ear... and without missing a beat, and with seconds left to spare, he seamlessly switched which part of the song he was singing! The band followed, the crowd followed and almost immediately the Mega-Christian-Musician-Big-Surprise happened and it was perfect.

All because the worship leader listened to what was being sung into his ear to get him back on track.

As I was riding along and listening to this story on the podcast, I kept wondering where this was going. What's the point he is trying to make here?

And then the pastor talked about how this is *exactly* what happens to us when we believe lies about ourselves. We fall out of sync with what God thinks about us and the truths He wants us to hold fast to. We need to allow God to "sing" us back on track. There's a beautiful song God wants us to sing, but we won't be able to hear it and join in if all we hear is the broken track of self-hatred that's been on repeat.

I'm not going to lie — that hit home for me so powerfully that I started crying. (Have you noticed a pattern yet? I cry a lot. It's my blurse... that stands for blessing/curse if you weren't aware of the words I've made up during my life.)

My whole life I experienced this tension between the head knowledge of "knowing" that God had made me beautiful, but feeling in my heart that I wasn't pretty.

I was stuck there because I wasn't allowing God to tell me that He loved me and made me wonderful and beautiful and unique. Instead, I was only telling myself that I couldn't be loved until I was "pretty." I was so off track.

It turned out that in all my seeking, what I actually needed was to be able to recognize the voice of the Shepherd so that I could hear Him sing me back to the place I need to be every time I wander and get off the beat. Jesus says in the gospel, "My sheep hear my voice and I know them and they follow me" (John 10:27).

My gut check moment was to ask myself, "If God is trying to get me back on track, do I even know what His voice sounds like and am I listening?" I wasn't sure that the answer was yes. And that scared me. I claimed to be a God-loving-girl, but I couldn't hear Him singing truth to me. I had work to do to learn what His voice sounded like.

It was time to try something new because I was exhausted from my quest for pretty. There had to be more. I had lost my place in the song and needed my Shepherd to guide me back.

I had made a false idol out of my own body. I was spending all my time and energy focused on how to make myself pretty and it was leading me to unhappiness. The very first commandment God gave us is that since He is the Lord, we should have no other gods, or false idols before Him. Rule number one and I couldn't even follow that one! But it's number one because it's important. In placing my bodily ideal as the number one thing in my life, I wasn't leaving that spot on the throne of my heart for God. I needed things to change if I truly believed that God deserved to be the Lord of my life and that I wanted to live to glorify Him and not myself.

So I dove head first into Scripture. I started praying more with God's words, learning them from the daily Mass readings, the Liturgy of the Hours, and by simply opening my Bible — mostly to the parts with Jesus in them. I love the Gospel of Luke so I often find myself reading about Jesus from that Gospel.

I went to my prayer time with the question most pressing on my heart, "What does it mean to be beautiful?" In these times of prayer, when I started to get the answers I was looking for, I was also reminded of women saints who lived lives of heroic virtue. People look back on them and talk about them as "beautiful" and I was drawn to that. Their lives are an example to us that we can learn from and I realized I was silly to not do all I can to remind myself of the lessons they can teach me. I also needed their prayers. I don't know what was always on the minds of the saints, but they couldn't have been focused on their outward appearance all the time or else they wouldn't have done such incredible things. The saints are talked about as "beautiful women of God" not because they got the perfect makeup on sale at Target. There's something more.

What I realized very slowly over time was that God never wanted "pretty" to be the focus of my energy. He didn't make us in order that we attain the goal of "pretty." He made us beautiful.

"You are altogether beautiful, my darling; there is no blemish in you" (Song of Solomon 4:7, NAB).

That is God's song.

That is the chorus He wants you to sing.

That is the place we need to be.

That is the truth to replace the broken track in your heart.

That is what He is whispering in your ear.

Once I started at that place with God and allowed Him to whisper that song to me when I got off track, everything began to change. I saw the world differently because I was first focused on God's song, and then I was trying to see the world with His eyes.

I learned that God defines true beauty much, much differently than the world defines it. These next chapters will each focus on one of the things God has taught me about beauty, and the things I'm doing daily to work toward focusing less on being "pretty" and more on seeing my beauty as a daughter of God.

This is how the Shepherd has helped me sing the right song. First, He sang love over me.

START WITH LOVE

I needed God to whisper His love into my life because a long time ago, I decided one thing about myself:

I decided that I couldn't stand myself since I wasn't pretty enough and that I will love myself "if... _____ ." And that sentence was finished with a variety of endings, depending on the year, the day, or my mood, but always it had to do with how "pretty" I felt. Often it sounded like one of the following:

I will love myself...

...if I lose weight...

...if I'm in a relationship...

...if I get 500 likes on Instagram...

...if I become a public speaker....

...if I am able to complete a half-marathon...

...if I wear the same size clothes as my sister...

...if, if, if... the list was never ending. The problem with all these statements is that they are conditions on how I will love and accept myself. That is just like saying to myself: you aren't good enough the way that you are. Be better.

It's saying that I'm not worthy of love and care as I am, right now. I'm only looking to some future version of myself and saying that when I get there, that's when things will change in my heart and mind and that's when I will finally love myself and be kind to myself.

But how flawed is that? How unlike God loves us? How counterproductive? In the midst of this self-loathing, I couldn't see how backwards it was to expect to improve myself and grow as a person while at the same time I was shaming myself for everything about myself.

One day I was sitting and praying with the Bible verse, "Love your neighbor as yourself" (Matthew 22:39). When I read the Bible I love to just linger on one sentence and let it sink in. God always has something new to reveal to us in Scripture, but I know often I've missed those things because I'm rushing through, reading too fast to "get it done" instead of taking my time to breathe in and ingest His Word. "Love your neighbor as yourself." As I read this verse over and over, praying for the

Holy Spirit to be present to me and inspire me as I prayed, those last two words hit me like a ton of bricks — "as yourself." I knew God was trying to reveal a truth to me in those two words.

I take loving my neighbor very seriously. Well, actually I haven't met the literal neighbor that lives next door to me yet, but I have given her a name and a life story, so that's a start. I named her Kate. She works in insurance and has a crush on a guy she works with named Matt, but she's afraid to say something because what if he doesn't like her back? To distract herself she goes to yoga and bakes. She looks like a Kate and if her name is in fact Kate, I will 100% faint from shock and awe and then retire in a cave as a prophetess.

Okay so besides (the girl whose name may in fact be) Kate, I do try to make a valiant effort to love those around me well. I try to smile, to say a kind word, to bake nice things, to be hospitable, to be a good listener, to offer encouragement to all those around me. I adore that St. (a.k.a. Mother) Teresa of Calcutta quote, "Let no one ever come to you without leaving better and happier. Be the living expression of God's kindness: kindness in your face, kindness in your eyes, kindness in your smile." I'm not a perfect example of living that quote, but I try very hard.

But how can I possibly live that quote out perfectly? How can I love my neighbor well if the qualifier for how to love your neighbor is how well you love yourself? The truth was that if I loved my neighbor as I loved myself, I would look at my neighbor and say, "You look ugly and gross today, you shouldn't have left the house." Or I would say, "I don't like you, or love you, or want to care about you... but be a size four and then we can talk."

Can you imagine? What kind of monster would I be? Could I honestly look at someone and say, "Your thighs jiggle weird and you can't even run four miles so you're the worst; you'll never be good enough." I could never say that to someone! I want to cry just imagining myself saying that to someone! It seems so contrary to my nature.

And yet that is exactly the kind of thing I was saying to myself.

When I read Matthew 22:39, I could not help but be honest with myself. I *don't love* myself as I deserve. I have put a million "conditions" on my love and acceptance of me. Conditions that may in fact be unattainable. I needed to reevaluate. I wasn't loving myself unconditionally, and it was preventing me from loving my neighbor fully and unconditionally.

I knew in my head that God loves me unconditionally, but that knowledge hadn't made it to my heart to really transform me. As much as I was putting conditions on how and when I would love myself, I was also extending that to my relationship with God. I was living in the lie that God didn't really love me unconditionally. I believed He would love me more if I was more pretty and more perfect.

I needed to fill my life with the knowledge and experience of God's unconditional love for me and let that love penetrate my heart. I needed to stop putting conditions on when and how I would love myself and start loving me for me. I couldn't imagine how much more of an overflow of love there would be in my life if I did that. If I accepted God's love for me in my heart, and started to love myself, then filled with that love it could overflow in abundance and I could share it with the souls around me.

I looked to how Jesus loved others to find an example of how He loves me. I found one in John chapter 4. Jesus showed us an incredible example of how to love unconditionally when He met the Samaritan woman at the well. If you're not familiar with the story, Jesus is travelling through the countryside and in the middle of the day He stops by a well where a woman is by herself getting water. Jesus is alone because He sent the apostles to go find food (because hangry is a real thing and no one wants a hangry Peter). So Jesus is there at the well with the woman and He asks her for a drink. This woman was not used to people talking to her because she was kind of a big deal in her town and not in a positive way. In fact, she was probably at the well in the middle of the day so that she wouldn't run into anyone else. She didn't want to see or talk to anyone. Bad timing, Jesus.

Or, maybe, *perfect timing.*

Jesus asks her for a drink from the well. She is surprised and a little unnerved because she is a

Samaritan woman and in Jewish law, anything she touched was considered impure and unlawful for a Jew to touch. And here Jesus was asking her if He could have a drink from the vessel she was handling. *Shocker #1.*

When the woman mentions how nuts Jesus is for asking her for a drink, Jesus responds by basically telling her, "Actually, you don't really know who I am and truthfully, people don't need this water, what everyone needs is the living water... which I have." Jesus then tells her to go get her husband.

At this point I imagine the woman looking down feeling a bit ashamed as she tells Him that she doesn't have a husband.

Jesus said to her, "You are right in saying, 'I have no husband'; for you have had five husbands, and he whom you now have is not your husband; this you said truly" (John 4:17-18).

But Jesus doesn't blink (I mean figuratively of course, because I can't actually vouch for the motion of Jesus' eyelids). He doesn't waver. He doesn't recant His offer to give her the living waters of eternal life. He doesn't get up and walk away because He only spends time with perfect (and/or pretty) people. Instead He does the opposite! He reveals even more to her! After another short exchange, it is recorded in John 4:25-26,

"The woman said to him, 'I know that Messiah is coming (he who is called Christ); when he comes,

he will show us all things.' Jesus said to her, 'I who speak to you am he.'"

Jesus hasn't been going around His whole life spilling this secret, you know. So the fact that the Gospel writer John included this one instance of Jesus' self-revelation is meant to tell us something.

God, who became a man named Jesus, wants us to know that we don't have to have it all together for God to be present to us... for Him to love us... and for Him to offer us the gift of the "living waters" of Baptism and the life of grace. God doesn't put the same conditions on His love that we put on His love. We are the ones who think we're not good enough, pretty enough, or sinless enough. We are the ones who attempt to push Him away with our litany of faults.

But to my soul He says, "My beloved, come to me and see the fullness of life. See who I am and how I love. See the love that I am constantly pouring out upon you."

God isn't waiting for us to achieve a certain condition before He loves us. He already sees us as beautiful. He sees us as His beloved children. He doesn't determine our worth by weighing our flaws and achievements...or by weighing us, period. Can you just imagine God asking everyone to step on the scale so that He could decide how He feels about us each day? That would be ridiculous! And yet that was what I was doing to myself! I was deciding how much or how little I would love myself on any given day based on the number on the scale, or how many zits I had on my face, or how well my hair did the thing I wanted it to do. I would only love myself if I was as pretty as that girl on Instagram modeling clothes for Urban Outfitters. I was making my love of myself all about the world's standard of perfection.

But... God's definition of beauty has nothing to do with the world's standard of what makes someone pretty.

Rather, beauty is written in our souls. It is inscribed in every fiber of our being.

Beauty isn't something we have to achieve; it is something God placed within us and we must discover within ourselves.

I am beautiful because God created me. I am beautiful because I am His daughter. I am beautiful because I am a human being, alive to bring Him glory. I am beautiful because I have a purpose on this Earth and He has a plan for my life. I am beautiful because I can be brave, and strong, and kind, and creative, and I can choose to love. I am beautiful because I can think intelligently and use my mind to learn about the world and about people and about my place in it all.

These aren't attributes that I see on the outside when I look in the mirror. This is much, much deeper than that. The beauty within me is more difficult to see if I haven't trained my eyes to see it. That's what I needed to fix, and the first step was to start to love myself for just being me.

In my quest to be pretty, I was so tough on myself that I only spoke negatively to myself and about myself. I couldn't see any of the good because I was so focused on what I saw as bad. God's unconditional love says "I love you no matter what," but my words and actions toward myself weren't echoing that.

I asked myself, what would it look like if I actually treated myself with love? What if I decided to never say to myself anything that I wouldn't say to my best friend, or my little sister? I wouldn't say to them the things I am willing to say to myself! And if anyone in my life deserves love and kindness, the first person must be me! After all, I spend the most time with me and, as I discovered, it gets awful dreary when I'm mean to myself all the time. Speaking with kindness and love toward myself, just as I would speak to my best friend, or little sister, would make such a huge difference in my life. And I deserve that. I deserve to be loved unconditionally by myself just as I want to love my neighbor unconditionally.

When I think about loving myself and others unconditionally, I'm reminded of one of my role models in this regard; her name was St. Agnes of Rome, who was a virgin and martyr in the year 304 AD.

She's essentially the exact opposite of the woman at the well. That woman was known in her town for being a bit promiscuous and having a bunch of different lovers. On the other end of the purity spectrum, Agnes vowed herself as a virgin bride of Christ and consistently denied the suitors who wanted to win her heart.

And let's talk for a minute about how she was um... 12 years old. (Maaaaaybe 13, but since she lived so long ago it seems the records aren't quite clear.) I don't know about you but when I was 12 years old I was not thinking about how my love relationship with God was my number one priority. I was thinking about how, "Oh my gosh my crush wants me to play video games again with him that must mean he's in love with me." Very un-Agnes-like.

This young girl was so amazing because no matter how often these guys bribed her with gifts, wealth, baskets of grapes, whatever else all the girls swooned over in 304 AD... she didn't budge. She was God's. She was His beloved and He was hers.

After a while this started to tick these guys off, so one of them reported her to the authorities as being a practicing Christian, which was against the law. Agnes... little, sweet, 12-year-old Agnes, was sentenced to be dragged through the streets naked and taken to a brothel! Only someone who really, really, really loves God and trusts Him could handle that. The legend has it that as she prayed, her hair grew super long and covered her nakedness and that, at the brothel, any man who tried to assault herwas struck blind. There's even one story that says a man who came to her at the brothel and tried to start something was struck dead in her presence! But she prayed over him and he was revived!

Since that punishment wasn't working, Agnes was killed by the sword and is one of those saints who has gone down in history as being the most willing victim ever. She couldn't wait to join God, her Beloved, in heaven! This world meant nothing to her. She had her whole life ahead of her but the anticipation of a life of earthly pleasures, a future of good food and fun and the joys of life, it all looked drab in comparison to being in heaven with her Bridegroom.

Little pre-teen Agnes was so in touch with who she was and why she was created. She knew the truth of her existence and every breath she took, every word she spoke, every prayer she uttered came from that place of deep-soul knowledge that she was loved. She knew. I can imagine her saying, "I am God's! I am loved by the God who created the heavens and the earth! He made the stars in the skies and the plants and animals on the ground, but He looked around and thought He needed me. He wants me! I am His beloved and He is mine! I am beautiful because I belong to God! And I am going home to Him!"

Wow. What would change in my life if I loved myself that way? What if I was so secure in who I am in God's eyes that I didn't doubt my beauty or my worth? What if I loved myself and my life like Agnes did so that I prioritized what is most important — my eventual union with my maker.

That would change my life. I would be *waiting* at the well to see if Jesus was going to come by. I wouldn't be consumed with my own faults, but I would be focused on Him and His love. All my actions would flow from that relationship — His love of me, teaching me to love myself, and letting that love spill over to those around me, my neighbors. I would be free to live my life in service of others because I could love them as much as I love myself. If I weren't looking in the mirror and finding my flaws, I would be less tempted to spot the flaws in others and commit harsh judgments in my mind. I would be free to live with heaven in mind instead of the pressures of this world weighing on my mind.

But it all starts with that love relationship with God. It starts with me reading about who Jesus is and accepting that He loves me just as much as the woman at the well. He loves me just as much as little Agnes. I am His little Christina. And I am the Samaritan woman, unworthy of His attention because of my sins. But still, I am His beloved through it all. I am still the one He looks upon as beautiful because I am His. And, like I imagine Agnes saying, I too can say, "I am God's! I am loved by the God who created the heavens and the earth! He made the stars in the skies and the plants and animals on the ground, but He looked around and thought He needed me. He wants me! I am His beloved and He is mine! I am beautiful because I belong to God! And (someday) I am going home to Him!"

Practically Speaking:

As I've been trying to practice this unconditional love of myself in my day to day life, here is what I've learned and what has helped me.

Write down affirmations of yourself, even if you don't initially believe them. Read them over to yourself. It might sound silly but, at one point, in order to "rewire" my brain in a sense, I had flashcards that had truths written on them. I would read through these flashcards every evening before bed. They said things like, "I am strong," "I am capable," "I am loveable," "I am beautiful." You can use all four of those, but I also would encourage you to come up with some that are specific to what you're feeling and going through.

Sometimes we just have to be practical to the point that it's almost funny. I sure felt silly reading these things to myself, but in some cases, I had never heard these statements about myself. I hadn't heard these specific affirmations from anyone else and I sure as heck hadn't ever said them to myself. So to say to myself that "I am beautiful" even if I was reading it from a flashcard, began to ingrain it in me. I needed to hear that I am beautiful not because of what I've done or how I look, but because it is a fact — that is how God created me. If you can't say nice things to yourself... try reading them to yourself first. Slowly you can record over that broken song of self-hatred with God's song of unconditional love.

PEOPLE NEED PEOPLE

One day, I looked in the mirror and I didn't hate my arms. That surprised me. Who was this person looking back at me and why wasn't she being her usual degrading self?

It was awesome! I didn't shudder and think my arms were huge and flabby and gross. I didn't go on and on for ten minutes chastising myself for being disgusting, or waste my whole day shrouded in gloom because I once again saw something that didn't satisfy my high expectations of perfection.

So what changed?

Nothing on the outside. I didn't lose a bunch of weight, or get a love poem from my crush that went on and on in perfect rhyming stanzas about how pretty I am. I hadn't gotten a record number of comments on an Instagram photo. Nope. I had simply gone out to coffee with a couple of my best friends.

Every Wednesday, I wake up before the sun. As soon as my alarm goes off, and every part of my body is alerted to how cozy and warm and perfect my bed is, I have to remember: people need people. I don't ever *really* want to leave that bed, but I'll put my feet on the floor knowing that I'm making a choice that is the best thing for my heart.

I hurry to get dressed and dash out the door, wiping the remnant of yesterday's makeup from the corners of my eyes as I head out to my car in the pre-sunrise darkness. On the drive I always blast my music as loud as I can handle to help wake me up, trying to force my body to forget that 4.2 minutes ago I was asleep in bed.

My friends and I all arrive at slightly staggered times, depending on who lives closest and farthest, and who gave in to the temptation of the snooze button. But what matters is that we're there... that we show up. Hugs get passed around as quickly and as pertinent as the steaming coffee warming our hands and scalding our throats. I look around the table at my best girl friends and I sit in wonder and awe at the beauty of each of them. All from such different walks of life, with different personalities, different features, and different stories to share about what has shaped their week and what state their heart is in today. Meeting weekly means we get to share about the little mundane things that fill our day to day lives. It also means we stay close to the stories of struggle that take time to play out in our lives. What one friend shares one week, she then updates us on as it plays out, week to week to week. I love that because we get to remind each other about how God is faithful and trustworthy, even when two months have gone by and nothing is resolved. We talk about Jesus and about love and mercy and grace and beauty. We also talk about lipstick, clothes, dating stories, and all the regular stuff girls talk about when you put two or more of them together.

Two or more. Does that ring a bell about what Jesus said about Christians getting together for fellowship and community? He said, "For where two or three are gathered in my name, there am I in the midst of them" (Matthew 18:20).

I think that's why it feels so sacred. As I sit there sharing coffee, laughter, tears, stories, and dreams with my best friends, I feel the hum of something holy. God is there. Even if we barely mention His name but to pray over our food and coffee, He is present. He is the love that we have for one another. He is the joy we feel in community. He is the truth that we share. He is the word we pass to one another when we say, "Have a good day, I love you. I'm praying for you." He is the beauty I see in my friends and they see in me.

I think that's why I went home from one of those coffee dates and looked in the mirror and saw my beauty instead of my flaws or the ways I wasn't "pretty enough." It's because being around my friends reminds me that I am more than my body. I am more than my exterior, whatever flaws or strengths I see in myself. When all of culture wants to tell me that I am only good enough if my body is perfect enough, my friends' love sends the contrary message that I am so desperately needed. I need those kinds of people in my life because they remind me that I am beautiful simply because I am me.

I've found that the relationships we build with people we love is one of the foundational building blocks to having a full, happy, healthy, and beautiful life. Isn't that exactly what Jesus did? Build close relationships with His friends? That's what I see all over throughout the Gospel stories! And whatever Jesus does should inspire us to take note for our own lives. This is the example of God being human. And God made real friends to spend time with.

One of my favorite stories of Jesus and one of His friends takes place after He has risen from the dead. The tomb is empty. Mary Magdalene is standing outside the tomb and, honestly, she was probably in shock. No matter how many miracles you see Jesus perform, you still don't think that He's going to rise from the dead, especially not after everyone saw Him beaten and nailed to a cross, and His mother holding His dead body in her arms. Mary Magdalene doesn't think that He's risen from the dead; she just thinks someone stole the body, which sucks. Her friend Jesus deserves the same amount of respect and dignity as anyone else, if not more! He was a leader, a teacher, a man with a following of disciples who were learning from Him. How dare they steal His body? She's upset. She's crying to herself outside the tomb when suddenly she turns around because there's someone there in the garden behind her. He says to her, "Woman, why are you weeping? Whom do you seek?" (John 20:15).

Mary is confused and thinks this man is the gardener, out and about and tending to the gardens around the tombs. This totally makes sense because even though Mary and Jesus were friends, once Jesus died and was resurrected, He was appearing in a "glorified" form of His body. I'm sure He didn't look the same as two weeks ago when He was covered in dust and dirt from travelling to Jerusalem and maybe hadn't had a haircut since He left His mama's house three years earlier. Mama wouldn't let Him get that scraggly look, but out on the road... a guys gonna do what a guys gonna do and that hair may have gotten as unruly as John-Living-in-The-Wilderness-Baptist.

Then Jesus says her name, "Mary."

She is immediately snapped out of her hysterics and she recognizes her friend once again. She replies by exclaiming, "Teacher!"

I can't even imagine how excited they must have been to see each other, especially after the traumatic events of the last couple days. But just as God always comes through and has a plan, He did this time, too, and things got better. Jesus rose from the dead, had reunions with His friends, shared meals and probably lots of laughter and storytelling, too.

What I learned from this beautiful exchange between Mary and Jesus is this: friendships are important. People need people.

Jesus recognizes what's going on with her when He approaches her. He sees her tears and how upset she is so He asks about it. He addresses the need of His friend. He calls her by name because they were friends as well as teacher and disciple. Jesus didn't write her off; He spoke to the deepest part of who she was by calling her by name. He dignified her by seeing her as who she was instead of seeing her as just another stranger.

We aren't meant to do life alone because we need those people who are going to remind us we are more and there's a bigger plan for our lives than just being perfectly pretty.

Like I said before, there are plenty of people and organizations who are ready to try and limit our dignity to what we look like. I can't help but think of St. Joan of Arc. Her whole story is incredible, but I want to focus on just one part of her story; the part where she's in jail after the whole, "lead everyone in war" thing even though she was a peasant girl. Joan got arrested and put in jail and then put on trial by a church court for being a heretic. It was absolutely unfair because the whole tribunal that was trying her were all English leaders, from the country she had been fighting against, so of course they hated her. She requested, as was the law, that some French leaders be put on the case too, but it never happened.

She went through many, many interrogations as they tried to find reasons to convict her of heresy and have her killed. Joan was brave and smart and faithful and all of her answers were perfect. They couldn't find a reason to convict her in her answers. Except they had one thing: she was wearing male clothing. While out on the battlefield she had been in a typical man's battle garb, and while in jail, though she didn't have her horse and shield and banner, she still wore male clothing. This made the court furious and they considered it heretical because it wasn't "proper and holy" for a young Catholic woman to dress like a man. (Yeah, so things have definitely changed... because when I wear jeans, no one even blinks an eye.)

But here's the thing... while in jail, Joan would've switched to wearing a dress... except that her guards kept trying to sexually assault her. She kept wearing the male clothing because it was more cover than a dress! It was a layer of protection because the outfit was held together by a lot of ties and hooks that were difficult to undo! Joan wasn't trying to be a man and deny her God-given femininity, she was trying to protect herself from men who only saw her as a pretty girl. They were objectifying her. She wasn't a beautiful person with a complex heart and mind... she was just a body to them, just a body that in their eyes was made solely for their pleasure.

What a nightmare. I was shocked when I learned this was part of St. Joan of Arc's story. I had only ever heard the war hero part! I mean, I had known she was burned at the stake, but I kind of assumed it was because she was a war prisoner.

Turns out that in the end, when the court couldn't find anything else wrong with her spirituality and practice of the Catholic faith, they focused in on her male clothes. She told people that she was wearing them because her guards were trying to sexually assault her, but they weren't listening to her. In the end, she was willing to wear a dress as long as she had a female guard assigned to her too. But her guards took away the dress and hid it, giving her only the male clothes. Once she put them on (to avoid being naked!!) they accused her once more of "relapsing" to her old ways of wanting to dress like a man. She was burned alive while tied to a stake on May 30, 1431, within days of that incident. She was only 19 years old.

What fortitude of spirit gets a girl through something like that? I struggle to wake up earlier on one day of the week and I complain about getting out of my comfy bed. And here we have St. Joan of Arc facing trial after trial and hours of interrogation all because she was only trying to protect herself from men trying to attack her and take advantage of her. So how did she stay strong? Besides her relationship with God, from which we are all able to draw the ultimate strength and grace, I think it was her relationships with her girlfriends that helped sustain her.

One of the other reasons she was on trial and being questioned was because she claimed that she had been having visions of St. Margaret and St. Catherine of Alexandria for approximately seven years, since she was about 12 years old. She said they were often talking with her, encouraging her, warning her, and supporting her in her faith. One particular time when she was in battle, they told her she would be captured, but to "take it in good part" because God would help her. During her interrogations, she said that St. Margaret and St. Catherine "often come without my calling, but sometimes if they did not come, I would pray God to send them." She also said, "I have never needed them without having them," meaning anytime she felt she needed their encouragement and support, they were there.

Don't you think they would have been there for her too all those nights alone in her prison cell, when she was afraid to go to sleep, afraid of which guard would come by and what they might do to her? Don't you think her girlfriends, St. Margaret and St. Catherine, were there to comfort her every time she walked out of an interrogation, dismayed that she wasn't getting a fair trial, and exhausted from the endless questions about her faith?

I'm sure they were because people need people. And whether that is a vision of a saint you can talk to, or a friend you can call and chat with or say "Hey, let's get coffee" ... it's important.

We aren't meant to get to heaven alone. We need friends and teachers and mentors and sisters. We need sisters who get it; who get how difficult it is to look in mirror and one day dislike what you see and the next day not care and the next day be able to say, "I'm beautiful," and then go through the cycle all over again. We need sisters who can encourage us when we feel like we're not good enough. We need them to tell us, like St. Margaret and St. Catherine said to Joan, to take everything in stride because God will help us.

I have a poster hanging in my house to remind me of this. It says:

"You'll need coffee shops and sunsets and road trips. Airplanes and passports and new songs and old songs, but people more than anything else. You will need other people and you will need to be that other person to someone else, a living, breathing screaming invitation to believe better things." *(Reblog Print, by To Write Love on Her Arms)*

For me, often times those "better things" I need my friends to invite me to believe is that I am beautiful and worthy simply because I am a beloved daughter of God. I need them to be around me in my highs and lows to love me through them so that I can know I am not loved based on how pretty I am, but I am loved because I am beautiful on the inside. And that's what matters after all.

That's why I get up before the sun on Wednesdays to sit and sip coffee with my best friends.... because people need people.

Practically Speaking:

If as you read this, you thought about *your* people — those girls who hold you up and keep you strong and remind you of your beauty, that's so great! If you're not already connecting with them often, start a group message with them and brainstorm some ways you can spend more intentional time together. Be it coffee like me and my friends do, or eating lunch together, or meeting at a park to walk and talk once a week, make it easy and comfortable and then ask your friends to really commit to it. Share your vision with them about how you want an even better friendship and see if they're on board. You don't have to have an agenda for these get togethers, just try to share the tough stuff, the stuff that's heavy on your heart, and what's going on with your relationship with God and your walk of faith. Those moments of sharing will naturally lead to a more powerful bond of friendship, and you'll go home feeling grateful... and beautiful.

If you don't already have those friends in your life, don't feel bad! It's not too late. God wants good things for you, and that includes good friends. Start to consistently pray that He places good friends in your life, and then be open to trying to meet those friends. You have to risk putting yourself out there and sharing who you are in order to begin to build relationships. It takes time and effort and some awkwardness. When you're behind a phone or computer screen, it's easy to think of the perfect thing to say. But in person, you have to risk saying some weird or stupid things. That's part of being human. And it's okay because even when we feel like we mess up or say awkward things, that can help reinforce in us that we are loved and valued and beautiful not for having it all together, but simply for being us (as authentic and awkward as we can be).

If you're not making friends at the places you already are every week, try joining a new club or taking part in a new hobby, going to free events for your age group through your town, or library, or community center. Volunteer your time somewhere that appeals to you, maybe it's a soup kitchen, or helping with babysitting ministry at a church, or helping teach a sport to younger kids. Also, get a job! I always made great friends with the people I worked with because we spent so many hours together, raking in that minimum-wage-dough! You have to get out there. Making friends takes time and you have to start somewhere. True friends will stand the test of time, but know that it's normal if you don't "click" with everyone. Each of our personalities don't mesh in that "best friend" kind of way with everyone, there's a little trial and error involved. You got this! Friends are a great blessing, and God will answer your prayer... so keep showing up.

CHILD, BE BRAVE AND SIMPLE

One of the problems I kept coming up against in my desire to be "pretty" was that I was overcomplicating everything. My mind always feels like it's running a marathon at sprint speed. Over and over I would circulate in the cloud of my mind all the things I thought would make me pretty, all the ways I wasn't achieving those things, and all the ways I wanted to be better, but also all the ways I was failing. Of course, let's not forget going over and over every word and action of my day to analyze it based on how people reacted to them or how they responded.

I wasn't singing to God's song of beauty because I was too busy fast forwarding, rewinding, and allowing my mind to replay the lies of the world on repeat.

What I needed was the breath of fresh air that simplicity can be.

For a God who literally knows everything, can do anything, and created everything, it is astounding to me that God's love is simple. He said it Himself: "Truly, I say to you, unless you turn and become like children, you will never enter the kingdom of heaven" (Matthew 18:3, RSV).

Does anyone else get a little scared reading that? Like, honestly Jesus, did you really mean to say that or you wanna take that one back? Jesus even uses the word "never." We'll never enter into the kingdom of God unless we become like little children.

And all this time I thought I had to become like a model to be beautiful. But God says no, beauty can be found in simplicity... like the simplicity of a child.

What I've learned from this truth is that there's beauty to be found inherently in children, and that one of the ways we can tap into that beauty is by tapping into the child we once were. At first to me it seemed impossible to get back to that place of childhood in our hearts. I thought I had grown too much, seen too much, read too much, and experienced too much to be that innocent and carefree. Isn't that what's beautiful about a child? Isn't their simplicity in the way they are innocent and clean? Unmarred by the pain and suffering of the world? Unaware of the potential dangers, threats, and violence that could be lurking around us?

When I was a child, my favorite place to be was outside. I remember my grandparents had this big wooden swing attached by thick chains to the biggest tree in the yard. The tree was at the top of a hill, and when I got on the swing to be pushed by my father, as the swing went up, up, up and out over the slope of the hill, I felt like I was a bird flying in the sky. My stomach would drop at the thrill of it. Fear didn't affect me, though, because nothing bad had ever happened on that swing. It was exciting and thrilling, but not scary. I didn't see any potential danger. I didn't know.

I didn't know sometimes people don't know how to push the swing as well as my dad did.

Sometimes people aren't smooth and constant, but rough and irregular as they push the swing.

Sometimes people will grab the swing as it comes back to make it stop suddenly, just to tease you.

Sometimes people are thinking more about how *they* can have fun than about how they can keep me safe.

Sometimes swinging over that hill could feel like you were launched off the edge of a cliff.

And sometimes, when things don't go right, when you get scared and confused and loosen your grip on the chains of the swing, a hard push will make you fall backwards and your skull will hit the ground with the force (but not quite the splatter) of a fly hitting the windshield of a semi truck on the highway. And that's exactly what happened to me one time.

I was shocked. Here I thought being pushed on that swing was a wonderful adventure! But now lying on the ground, my head throbbing in pain and tears running down my cheeks, pooling in my ears and soaking my hair... I knew the truth: the swing is a mean, dangerous thing. I didn't want anything to do with that swing.

It was like a little piece of my childhood innocence was ruined that day. After the experience of pain and suffering that the swing could potentially cause, that was all I thought of when I saw that swing for awhile. I couldn't imagine getting back on it and choosing to risk the potential pain for the chance at a little joy and freedom.

I think that experience repeated itself over and over again throughout my life. The things I thought were awesome (and fun, exciting, thrilling, adventurous...) would at one point cause me pain. Then I would live in fear of that thing, wanting to avoid it in order to stay safe. This happened with making friends, going to birthday parties, climbing trees, having a crush on a boy, buying new clothes, participating in contests... you get the idea. Eventually all things that I thought were harmless and fun turned out to disappoint me in some way. It made me want to withdraw into myself; I wanted to hide from life in order to not have to deal with things hurting me. I grew jaded. And I related all of it to me not being good enough. If other people could keep going on and enjoying life, what was different about me? There had to be something wrong, and of course, I always related it back to my looks. I had decided I wasn't pretty. That's why I was rejected by friends, boys, social groups, and even trees that ejected me from their limbs. Maybe it was silly to relate it all, but in my mind I only built up all the reasons I wasn't good enough, and not being pretty always made it into the pile of reasons.

There's the story in the Bible of a girl named Sarah who was in a similar position. She was afraid of life and going on with her life because of all the pain she had experienced.

You see, Sarah was a young woman whose life (initially) was going great. She was at the age to get married, which for a young woman in that time meant that they were starting a life on their own! Now she got to help manage a house, and love a husband. I'm sure she was excited for this new life of hers to begin. She may have also been a little nervous to get married, but overall, I imagine that it was a positive experience in her mind. I like to imagine her thinking, "This is what women do! This is the start of my new life!"

But then the unthinkable happened. On her wedding night, while I'm sure her guests were still off drinking and having a grand 'ole time... Sarah and her new husband went off to consummate their marriage and he died suddenly! What was supposed to be a happy, wonderful day, turned into a nightmare for Sarah. Their guests had to go from celebrating a wedding one day to mourning the loss of the groom at a funeral the next day.

I wonder how long it took Sarah to heal from that tragedy? When there have been deaths in my family or among my friends, sometimes it takes me weeks, months, or years to process it and move on. I know God will take care of their souls, but I need time to mourn and get on with living my own life. But for Sarah, it wasn't just a distant relative, this was the man she was ready to spend her whole life with. Plus, he didn't die while off in a foreign land... he died in their bedroom on what should have been one of the happiest days of her life. Talk about scarring.

But she got over it somehow. She was able to move on. Eventually she was ready to be married again and her father gave her hand in marriage to another man. A new start. A fresh life. The newlyweds were happy, and the past pain had faded to a quiet whisper of a memory.

And he died. Her second husband met the same fate as her first. On the night after they were given to each other in marriage, he died in the bedroom and Sarah was widowed a second time. Another grave. Another round of mourning. What could be worse?

I'll tell you what could be worse... it didn't just happen twice; it happened another five times! Sarah was married to seven men, all of whom died on their first night together. This poor woman's life was racked with sorrow and death. Seven marriages. Seven chances at joy. Seven men she watched die in front of her. Seven graves.

After she went through all that, Sarah wanted to die herself. She was so raw from the wounds caused by her tragic marriages that when one of her father's servants made fun of her for what her life had become, Sarah became suicidal. She thought it would be better if she just escaped the pain of the world, the memory of seven husbands dying in front of her, and the view of seven graves. Hanging herself seemed like the best option. However, because she loved her father and didn't want his name to be further disgraced she didn't hang herself. Instead she prayed that God would just take her life. God didn't do that. Instead He sent her one more husband — an eighth. His name was Tobit and he had loved her since he had first heard about her from the mouth of an angel named Raphael.

I can just imagine her father and mother lamenting to each other, "Here it goes again… can we handle one more wedding ceremony? One more death? One more round of trauma, heartbreak, and mourning for Sarah?"

They gave Sarah's hand in marriage to Tobit. And then Sarah and her mother went to prepare the bedroom for the night. Sarah's mother wept. Maybe she was filled with dread and sorrow for her daughter. But she also had a little hope. She said to Sarah, "Be brave, my child; the Lord of heaven and earth grant you joy in place of this sorrow of yours. Be brave, my daughter" (Tobit 7:18).

I *love* that line. Absolutely love it. Those are the words that I need to hear so often when my childlike innocence is nowhere to be found and all I see around me is pain, suffering, or the potential of it. Be brave. God can do all things, even replace sorrow with joy.

Sarah's mom said those words and in the meantime Sarah's father had his servants go out and dig another grave, an eighth grave ready for the body of Sarah's eighth dead husband. They had a shred of hope, but were also prepared for the worst.

But God was merciful. He answered their prayers and Tobit, Sarah's new husband, did not die like the rest. History did not repeat itself again. There was newness. Sarah had been brave and persevered in her faith. She didn't give up when she wanted so desperately to end her life because of the cycle of pain and suffering she had gotten caught up in.

I think Sarah would have had moments like we all do… like I did every time I realized the things I was excited about and that I thought were harmless actually were capable of causing me great pain — like falling off the swing which I thought was perfect and could only bring me joy. Sarah thought marriage would bring goodness into her life, more joy and more peace, not more pain and trauma. It happens to all of us. No wonder we all feel like as we grow up our childlike nature and innocence is gone forever.

But if Jesus said that we must be childlike to enter into the kingdom of heaven, He has a way for us to reconnect with our childlike heart, a path to find our way to the beauty of a simple soul.

I think that way is brave trust. If every word of the Bible is the word of God, then that verse, "be brave my child," is what He is saying to you and to me! This is another one of God's songs that He has whispered to my heart to get me back on track. When I'm feeling scared and tired of life letting me down... when I feel like everything will end in pain and suffering... when I feel like I'm never going to be good enough, or I'm never going to live day to day realizing how beautiful God created me and living in that beauty, God whispers, "be brave my child" and those words revive in my heart the trust and surrender and joy of what it's like to be a child, trust my father to guide the going out and coming in of the swing, the pendulum of my life and it's ebb and flow.

There's one saint who has taught me the most about how beauty is simple and childlike is: Chiara Luce Badano. Ever since I came across this young saint's story, I haven't been able to forget it. It's a story that I know as well as any fairy tale, embedded forever into my memory because it was so moving to me.

Chiara lived in the 1970's, the same time my parents were in high school! That in and of itself is crazy to me. There are people who have become and are becoming saints in this century we are living in! Doesn't that give you so much hope? I really, really love saints I can relate to and Chiara is one of them. She loved tennis and being outside and hanging out with friends! And she didn't always do well in school. Same, Chiara. Same.

She was known for being super joyful and kind; everyone wanted to be around her. When she was a young teen, she discovered she had an incredibly painful case of bone cancer. She suffered for a couple years and then died from it when she was only 18 years old.

What struck me the most about her life and what has left a lasting impression on me, is the way she simplified holiness. She loved Jesus so much that all she wanted was to live for Him and to show His love to others. That's it. She didn't overcomplicate it. She didn't write a bunch of diaries or do a ton of charitable work. She loved joyfully and that love and joy spilled over onto everyone near her. One time her mom asked her if she talks to her friends about Jesus. She told her mom that no, she doesn't have to talk to them about Jesus because it's more important that she "give Him to them" by the way she listens, dresses, and by the way she loves them. Mic drop.

She also had a huge heart for the poor and her whole life, even up until her death, she kept a list of all her belongings so that she would know what she had on hand to give away if the opportunity arose.

As she was dying, suffering great pain from the cancer in her bones, she would often completely refuse to take strong pain medications like morphine because it would impair her mental clarity and make it more difficult for her to be present to offer her sufferings to God.

And here I am popping Excedrin at the slightest suggestion of a headache. I can't believe how far I have to go when I read about people like Chiara.

One thing I'm fascinated by about "modern-day saints" is that we actually have good photographs of them! So as soon as I started learning about Chiara, I Googled her to see photos of her and holy wow:

She. Is. Gorgeous.

Like glowing, radiantly beautiful. There's something other-worldly about her eyes and her smile. It's like she has a secret (but not in a Mona-Lisa creepy way).

If you were to judge Chiara by popular beauty standards, she wouldn't measure up very well, I'm sure. She isn't the stereotypical model kind of pretty... she has the beauty of a saint. Her beauty radiates from within, it's not something only seen on her exterior. In fact, as she was undergoing cancer treatment and her hair was starting to fall out, every time she lost a hair she would look at that hair and simply say, "For you, Jesus." What a simple bravery. What a beautiful childlike prayer.

She didn't agonize over every hair. She didn't complain. She didn't worry what others would think. Or at least her words and demeanor made it seem like she didn't allow herself to dwell on those things. Instead she surrendered to what God was allowing her to go through and she offered it back to Him.

Chiara's surrender of her life, her possessions, her pain, and even her physical looks to God is such an inspiring example to me what it means to be like a simple child. I want to be more like her.

Her whole life was an embodiment of the prayer: "Here Dad, all of my life is yours, take it all." She gave Him her heart and He brought her safely home to His arms.

Beauty is found in simplicity, the simplicity of a child. The trust and surrender of a heart that knows they are in good hands. A heart that believes that whatever may come, whatever heights they fly to or falls they may take, whatever pain there may be in life, we have a Father whose only concern is to love and care for us, each of us as His individual daughters.

"Be brave my child."

Those are the words God is whispering to us in our moments of fear and doubt. And like a child who knows where to turn, may we always take those fears and doubts to our Father. This is what makes us beautiful. When the world is telling us to worry about what others will think, and to do everything we can to be better and prettier than the next girl, a childlike heart can see the folly of it all because all she wants is to be beautiful for her Father, and He already made her so.

Practically Speaking:

This will take time. As we grow up we get used to fending for ourselves. We realize that no one knows us like we know us. So we take care of me, myself, and I because we know what's best. Or do we? Saint Augustine in his "Confessions" wrote that God is, "higher than my highest and more inward than my innermost self." God knows us better than we know ourselves. He knows our fears and our hopes, the ways that we sin, and the reasons behind our sin. He knows how you've been hurt, betrayed, and why you've put some walls up around your heart.

So you can trust Him with it all. One of the things I've been doing to help me surrender to God is to make a list in my journal of all the things that are on my mind and causing me to fear, or be worried, stressed, or anxious. Then I cross out the things that are outside of my control. Like, "my friend might be jealous that I got a new car before her." I can't control how my friend feels, so it's not worth worrying about. It gets crossed off. Then I cross off the things that I need to trust God with. "Return my grossly overdue library books" is not something I need to trust God with. I need to just get that done. But "I'm afraid I'll never find love" is an anxiety that I can put in His hands so I cross it out because it's not up to me to worry about that one, it's up to God. Thirdly, on the list of items that are left, I try to see what practical steps I can take to alleviate the worry they are causing. What day will I take my books back? Tuesday. Done. Not a stress factor anymore.

It's a wonderful practice that I do over and over, sometimes once a week, sometimes once a month, to help me make sure I'm reminding myself to be brave and trust God with the things in my life that I can surrender to Him. He knows you. He gets your heart. And He's on your side. Try making your list. I think you'll be surprised how many stresses and fears in your life you can put in His hands instead of turning them over in your mind. This practice leads to a more simple and trusting faith — which is beautiful.

REALITY STARS AND RADICAL HONESTY

Have you ever heard of a girl called "Honey Boo-Boo"? Actually, her real name is Alana, but her popular nickname is Honey Boo-Boo. She is a young girl who, as a child, participated in toddler beauty pageants. She has a huge personality and after being in a couple pageants and gaining the attention of the media, she and her family were given their own reality TV show. Now I could say a million things about the show, but let me just say this one disclaimer: there was a lot of brokenness in their family and a lot of ways that they were not great models of family life.

However....

What I loved about Honey Boo-Boo was her blatant, radical honesty. It was addicting to watch this girl's life because she said what all of us were thinking! And more! It's also what made her hilarious to watch. Her commentary on everyday life was priceless.

She had a bit of a gut on her and she liked to grab all of it in her hands and shake it up and down and pretend to make the "rolls" in her tummy talk. It's so funny to watch! And those of us with a bit of a gut could use some of her humor when looking in the mirror!

She is also unabashedly addicted to cheese puffs — you know those crunchy balls that leave a cheesy residue all over your hands as soon as you take one handful? She loves them so much that when her sister gave birth to a baby who had an extra finger on one of her hands, Honey Boo-Boo said that the baby was so lucky and she wished she had an extra finger because she would use it to grab more cheese puffs! In doing pageants, she knows that she's a diva, and she knows exactly why she does it — "dolla' makes me holla'" she tells the camera. I remember another clip where she was holding a bouquet of flowers and a little hand mirror, twisting it back and forth from the flowers to herself saying, "You're pretty and you're pretty and you're pretty and you're pretty!" to both the flowers and to herself in the mirror.

Alana was so upbeat, so positive. She was sure of herself. She knew who she was and what she loved and what made her awesome. She was less than ten years old but I, as a 20-something, envied her self-esteem and self-confidence. I also appreciated her honesty about herself and her observations about life.

When I look around me, I don't see that honesty very much. I think that's partly what drew me to her TV show. I was recently talking with a friend about social media and how it's tough to approach social media with a balanced point of view and wisdom because, since it's real people sharing their lives, it's hard to remember that they are also showing the best part of their lives, the edited version of their lives. Some people are using apps to alter their photos to make them look thinner and to smooth out their skin. They're twisting their bodies into poses that accentuate what they want. They are only showing the world their highlights. It's not real life. Those social media queens who may look like normal people but are getting hundreds of thousands of likes per picture are not showing us their low moments. We don't see the times they feel depressed because no one has texted them back or when they're heartbroken over a breakup. Social media hasn't become the place for honesty — it's a place for masks.

That's not the honesty that I saw in a little eight-year-old pageant queen. And that's not the honesty that builds self-esteem. Whenever I've been on social media presenting the best, prettiest, most organized, always-ready-for-a-party version of myself, I actually feel less self-worth after I get a ton of likes. I feel less beautiful because I know that the version of "me" I just put on social media isn't the real me that I live with 95% of the time. And if it's the 5% that 502 people just "liked" … will they even like the real me? Am I likeable? Am I lovable? Am I beautiful?

The litany of doubts starts all over again.

But I fight it with honesty. Honesty helps me discover my inner beauty. It is in honesty that I can face who I really am as a daughter of God — flaws and all. When I'm honest with myself I look at my imperfections squarely and accept them for what they are.

Honesty leads me to see my beauty because it helps me gain self-esteem. And feeling great about who I am, feeling secure as a daughter of God — that helps me to see my God-given beauty.

Radical honesty with myself means that I have to face up to the fact that sometimes I don't pray enough. It means I have to admit that I don't always achieve the goals I set and that it's my own laziness that's to blame. I have to admit that sometimes I want followers and likes on social media instead of wanting real relationships. I need to admit that I don't eat well sometimes, I don't exercise as much as I would like to, and that I am carrying some extra pounds on my body.

That's not fat-shaming myself, it's being honest with myself. And when I look at my life with radical honesty, I don't feel bad! I actually feel freed because I'm not hiding it all anymore. I feel empowered to set goals to do something about it because I love and appreciate myself. It doesn't come from a place of hate fueled by comparison. When I am ready to be honest, it comes from a place of care. There's a difference between seeking out your faults because you want to tear yourself down and recognizing your flaws because you're ready to make yourself better. Once you know how much God loves you and you're living in that love, when you're letting Him sing that song of love over you, and you start to love yourself, that's when you can be lovingly, radically honest.

One of the quotes that motivates me was written by St. Irenaeus. He said, "The glory of God is man fully alive."

What does it mean to be fully alive? It means to live well as a whole person, and not just in one area of who we are as people. You see, God didn't just make us as souls and then stick the soul in a body. Nor did He make a body as something separate from a soul. Nope. We are what's called an "integrated being" and we are equally body and soul. The human named Christina Mead is a body/soul person. What I may think I'm just doing with my body, I am doing as a whole person with my soul as well. Therefore, to be fully alive and to give glory to God in that, I want to have a healthy soul, a healthy mind, and a healthy body.

Being fully alive or at least working towards the healthiest, holiest version of myself, makes me a happier person. I am more energetic, positive, and thoughtful when I am healthy. I am also more in tune to what God is doing in my life. I can hear Him better, see Him clearer, and pray more easily. I am able to be more aware of my inner beauty. In taking good care of myself I remind myself of my worth.

It reminds me that I am precious and I am worth caring for!

We have to look out for our basic needs before we can reach higher goals. For example: If you're not getting food every day, you won't be able to contribute to society by having a job. You wouldn't have the energy for it. If we don't take good care of our bodies, our whole being is affected. Being honest about the health of our whole person is one of the key foundations to growing in self-esteem in order to recognize our inner beauty.

Jesus talked about this, too. As Jesus was gaining attention in His ministry, He was also gaining quite a crowd of people who wanted to follow after Him and be His disciples. At one point, He says to them:

"For which of you, desiring to build a tower, does not first sit down and count the cost, whether he has enough to complete it? Otherwise, when he has laid a foundation, and is not able to finish, all who see it begin to mock him, saying, 'This man began to build, and was not able to finish.' Or what king, going to encounter another king in war, will not sit down first and take counsel whether he is able with ten thousand to meet him who comes against him with twenty thousand? And if not, while the other is yet a great way off, he sends an embassy and asks terms of peace" (Luke 14:28-32).

Then He says that in order to be His disciple, you have to surrender everything or else you'll be a half-hearted disciple. Jesus was teaching that crowd of disciple wanna-be's, and He's teaching us that if you want something, if you have an end goal, then you have to take a look at what you've got, what you need, and how you're going to get there. Those new-fangled nerds call it "self-awareness." We can use that word, or we can also call it honesty.

Jesus is being super practical, which is awesome to me because it's easy to make everything Jesus says seem very spiritual, other-worldly, and hard to grasp. But here He's talking in MY language — my practical, list-making mind loves this kind of Jesus-talk.

Take a look at what you have and what you need before you start to build something. Count your troops and arm yourself correctly before you go to war against the bad guys.

Apply that to your life.

Find out the root causes of your low self-esteem before you begin to heal that self-esteem. Arm yourself with truth before you go to war against the culture that says you have to look physically perfect to be beautiful.

There are steps to follow. Even Jesus Himself gave us this advice. And, to me, that advice is freeing because it means that Jesus understands we're not quite there yet. He understands there is self-awareness, or honesty, that's needed when we look at our own lives before we can move on to the next step.

For me, I had to be honest that if I wanted to constantly feel confident in my inner beauty, it meant that I had to grow overall in self-esteem. What did I need to do to grow in self-esteem? There were things that needed to get cut out of my life. There were things that needed to be added to my life. There were people I needed to see less of, and other people I needed to see more of. I had to look at all the areas of my life and in moments (which were totally fueled by grace) of radical honesty, I could see what was helping me to be more fully alive, and what wasn't. Jesus wanted me to move forward in my journey as a disciple who could listen well to His voice, but I had to let go of some things.

Any time it's difficult for me to do that, God likes to remind me of one little part of the story of St. Teresa of Avila's life. Can I just say first of all that every time I think I have nothing in common with the saints, I am always, always, always proven wrong. Sometimes you just have to dig deeper than the children's storybook version of the saints' lives.

When I read more in depth about St. Teresa of Avila, I was astonished to find out that this saint, known for reforming the Carmelite Order of religious sisters, seemed like a really normal young woman.

She liked fashion, jewelry, books — most especially romance novels... can't you just imagine young 17-year-old, Teresa from Spain walking through the streets of Avila clutching her book to her heart and singing, "Far off places, daring swordfights, magic spells, a prince in disguise!" just like Belle in Beauty and the Beast? Besides her romance novels she also liked attention, especially from men. Her father noticed that she was interested in all these things so he decided the best place for her would be the monastery. Isn't that every dad's dream come true? To hide his daughter away from the world to pray and grow in virtue until they die and become saints, never marred by the heartbreak of love?

Well unfortunately for Teresa's father, the monastery actually wasn't that different from normal life outside the monastery. The nuns still wore jewelry to spruce up their habits, and they still were able to have tons of guests all the time. Prayer? What prayer? Teresa didn't give it much thought since she was busy hanging out, gossiping, and generally having a grand 'ole time with friends and visitors. She was popular too, so everyone wanted to be around her.

After a couple years, things started to change for Teresa when she was challenged by a priest to take her prayer time more seriously. At first, Teresa did so begrudgingly; prayer was a chore and when she went to pray she would just wait for it to be over. And when you think about it, that's not surprising at all. It's tough to begin to pray and listen and communicate with God when you're used to only talking with young and lively men and women who can't wait to hang out with you and tell you the latest gossip.

But she kept at it and slowly her heart began to fall more and more in love with God. She longed to unite herself even more to Him, and to focus her life on being His.

It became time to evaluate her life. She wanted something new and different. She wanted a greater union with God as a religious sister who had given her life to Him. Now it was time to decide what needed to happen in order to have that greater union. For Teresa, it meant that she needed to cut out what wasn't serving the bigger goal in her life. The first big thing she chose to do was to spend a lot less time socializing in the monastery parlor with the visitors and her friends. For her, she knew it wasn't helping at this time in her spiritual life. It had been shallow and she was ready to enter deeper into the spiritual life.

Now remember, this was the popular girl whom everyone loved. She had the recognition and affirmation of many people to validate her and make her feel worthy and beautiful. But she wanted God. How tough it must have been to pull away from that attention! And her friends didn't make it any easier. They were actually pretty mean about it. They are started gossiping about her and even sent a priest to "evaluate" her spiritual life to see if she had gone crazy.

"Crazy" because she didn't want for herself the life they wanted for her. Some friends they were.

When I hear stories like this, I can't help but wonder about the other details that we don't read about.

My imagination fills in the gaps with what I know about what it's like to be a girl in these situations. I bet it was so hard for Teresa to make that decision and then stick to it when everyone was mad at her and saying mean things about her. It really stinks when the people you thought were your friends won't support what you're doing, especially when it is for your overall spiritual good. She wanted to be fully alive and enter more fully into her relationship with God, but she was misunderstood. That would make anyone want to abandon their resolve!

I imagine her going to God in prayer and saying, "This is so tough, I thought they were my friends but they won't support me in wanting to spend less time having 'fun' and more time in prayer!" The honest truth was that they couldn't see what was best for her. Only she could see that. Only she knew what she needed. I'm sure she had lots of days when she would have rather said, "You know what everyone, never mind, you're right, I just want to hang out and talk about the newest rumors, and can someone go buy me that cheese danish that I love? Okay, gracias."

She didn't say that, though. Instead, she held to what she had discovered about herself in a moment of radical honesty and she put more prayer and less shallow socializing in her life. She had the bravery to say "Not this, I choose something different, something more."

And now we call her a saint.

That's the power of honesty! That's the power of looking at what we have in our lives and evaluating it based on where we want to go.

I knew deep down that I wanted to be fully alive in order to give glory to God so I had to look at my life and say, "I need more prayer time in Adoration of the Eucharist. I need to move my body more. I need to eat better. I need more fruitful community in my life — friends who care about my soul more than anything else. I need to take care of these basic things in order to reach something better and higher." In taking care of those things, I started to have a better self-esteem because with everything I was doing, I was affirming that I was worth it. I am worth the effort. I am worth taking care of. I am worth setting goals for my life and achieving them in order to keep growing in self-esteem and feeling better about myself.

The courage to look at our lives squarely and honestly and assess how we're doing and how we want to change is a beautiful virtue. It takes guts to say, "not this" about where we are. It's that self-awareness that Alana (a.k.a Honey-Boo-Boo), Jesus, and St. Teresa of Avila had (I can't believe I have those three in a sentence together).

I've learned that beauty is honest; false masks will never give us freedom from the negative cycle of self-hatred. When I look at my life, my spirituality, and my body in honesty, I unlock a beauty within me that couldn't be seen under the false pretense of "having it all together." And I'm so grateful for that.

Practically Speaking:

This is going to be tough — to look honestly at your life and assess where you are and where you want to go. I promise it's a process that will help you grow in self-esteem and find and know your beauty on a deeper lever!

So the first step is to take some time alone and think about the different dimensions of who you are: mind, body, and soul. What are you doing well in those areas? What aren't you doing well? What goals do you have for those areas? And what needs to change? What is the most difficult thing to let go of if you want to change? Why is it difficult? What positive thing or habit could you replace it with?

Make a list of goals and then break them down into what you can do weekly, monthly, and what you want to accomplish in a year, then in five years. Be sure to make them practical and easy to measure. "Be more holy" is a tough goal to measure. Try instead: "Go to Confession every month." Also, be sure to make your goals manageable and if you're unsure if they're too big, ask a friend or mentor that you can trust to be honest with you. "Lose 30 lbs in 30 days" is not healthy, but "exercise four times a week" is much more balanced and wise.

ROYALS IN THE KINGDOM

Isn't it weird to go to a restaurant? Really though, think about it for a minute. You walk up to the place and demand, "Table for two!" You're led through the restaurant like you're the grand finale of a mini-parade in your honor. Once seated, this is your domain. You get to dictate everything to your ~~servant~~ server who is there to ~~bow down~~ wait on you. More water! Less ice! Cleaner utensils! New appetizers! Medium-rare, not medium-well steak! Bring me a bowl of ranch dressing, this tiny receptacle is unacceptable.

We get what we want and make a mess and then ignore any responsibility for our actions by leaving it all for someone else to clean up. It actually feels like we're royalty (at least to me). I suppose that is great because if I'm ever not feeling beautiful, all I have to do is go to a restaurant to hopefully be treated like a queen, then I'll feel great about myself again. I can walk out of that restaurant and proclaim on the street corner, "I'M AWESOME" because only awesome people can demand entire bowls of ranch dressing and have their wishes fulfilled.

It's weird. And incredible.

I'm going to choose to think it's a good thing to feel like royalty sometimes because, actually, I think it might be a good reminder about how we need to be living our spiritual lives like the Kingdom of God is here and now – because that's what Jesus said and what the New Testament writers affirmed.

Jesus kept saying throughout the Gospels that the Kingdom of God is here. It is now. It is among us. But what does it mean?

It means that if we have been baptized and welcomed into the family of God, we've also been invited to see the glory of Christ's Kingdom all around us and live in that Kingdom today in the here and now.

When God created the world, as we read about in Genesis chapters 1 and 2, He made everything to be in this beautiful state of harmony and blessedness. The world wasn't at odds against itself. There was no sin and no death. There were no lies saying that in order to be considered "beautiful" you had to be "this" size, or wear "these" clothes from "this" designer" and your hair should be "this" color and style and your skin should have "this" many imperfections (hint: zero). There were no lies about us not being good enough. Innocence never died.

Fear wasn't a thing.

But we know what happens right after the creation of the world in Genesis chapter 3. Everything falls apart. Sin enters the picture. Death enters the scene. There is brokenness and destruction and pain and suffering and instead of the earth being in union with the Divine, a chasm is created.

But God (of course, because He's just great) had a plan to restore all things back to Him and that plan was Jesus. God became man and what did He do while He was here on earth? He started renewing and restoring and reconciling the world back in union with the Divine. Water turns to wine at His hands. The blind see again, and the lame walk. He brings dead people back to life.

And then, as the big capstone of His earth trip, after they torture Him and hang Him on a cross like a criminal and He dies, He *Himself* comes back to life. The grave is empty. Jesus Christ resurrected from the dead reunited our world with the Divine once again. This is the Good News: that, though we were dead in sin, we can now be united with God, alive again in a restoration of our original relationship with Him.

This is what Jesus meant when He said the Kingdom of God is here.

In Genesis 1 and 2 we read that as God surveys the heavens and the earth and humanity He says, "It is good." And now we live in a world post-resurrection where "it is good" once again through the power of grace! This world isn't something we have to escape; we can enter in and experience the Divine here among us.

But it takes our participation. We have to choose to be a part of the new creation that Jesus came to restore. You and I know all too well what it's like to still experience the brokenness of the world. There's still hatred and greed and sin and often I see it in my own heart, first and foremost. We need God's redeeming grace every moment of every day. We need the sacraments. We need the forgiveness of the Sacrament of Reconciliation. And then we need it again, and again, and again. And each time we choose to participate with grace and enter into the reality of the Kingdom of God in the here and now, we will experience more grace, meaning, and beauty in all of the people and places and things around us because all of it is God's! God has redeemed the world and creation, including us, and so there is good we can find in our world and that we can experience – and God is continuing this work of perfecting the world until one day all is restored in a new heaven and new earth.

Will you choose to enter in and see it? Will you participate with grace and live in union with God? It means that everything about our daily life can be holy. Waking up, the feel of the warm sheets, the sound of the alarm, the smell of warm toast and butter, sliding into your shoes, the sun coming through the windows with that warm morning glow... or on the flip side -- the sound of the rain and the whoosh of the wind and way the clouds hang low and dark as if they're holding us close, hiding us under a blanket and protecting us. The way the neighbor accidentally slams her door as she's shutting it every day. The small talk with the UPS man. The sound your little sibling makes every night as they tap their fork on the table trying to avoid eating their vegetables.

It's holy. It's sacred. All of what we think of as just "normal life" actually reverberates with spiritual significance and the sublime glory of God. We are part of the restored Kingdom of God. It is here among us because Jesus conquered death! Jesus Himself took part in those ordinary day to day things too.

I love the story from John 21 after Jesus has been resurrected from the dead and He goes to the seashore to find some of His apostles, who had gone right back to their lives of fishing as if the three years with Jesus didn't even happen. First, Jesus tells them where to put their nets and they catch a boatload of fish. A literal boatload. The boat was loaded. So first they are astounded about that and then they come to the shore and Jesus has breakfast with them — which is the part that astounds ME because I love breakfast too! And here we have the Gospel writer John including the fact that Jesus too appreciated breakfast and the need for it and glory of it.

The glory of it. The day to day ordinary glory of the things of this Earth. Jesus didn't scoff at "worldly things" like bread and fish and sitting on the ground chatting with His friends. He entered into it all because it's all apart of His Kingdom, and it is good!

We are currently members of His kingdom. We are royals — sons and daughters of the King. This is good news because it means that this life on Earth isn't just about trying to get by and see how quickly we can get it over with and get to heaven to be in God's Kingdom there. If all this life down here is sacred too, then we'd be missing out on something important if we only took things for their face value.

When we sharpen our focus on seeing and grasping and living the reality of the Kingdom of God in the here and now, we see that God has left us pieces of His beauty all around us. If you can see the beauty around you, the beauty that speaks to your soul of a God who is bigger and more beautiful than we can imagine... then you can more easily see the beauty within you.

Remember, our own feelings about our beauty can't be isolated from the rest of who we are. We are integrated beings and each area of our lives can have an affect on other areas of our lives. Seeing beauty around you trains you to see it in the face in the mirror.

I'm tempted only to see my flaws when I look in the mirror, but there's more to me than a body with some imperfections. I am an eternal being! And you are too. Our hair, our skin, our eyes, our thighs that may be a little rounder or a little too skinny — all of it is part of who we are — eternal beings that are invited to be a part of God's Kingdom forever.

When all I do is stress about how I look, I'm missing out on the bigger picture. I am more. And so are the people and events and nature around me.

I love the story of St. Elizabeth of Hungary and what she's taught me about the sacredness of who we are in the Kingdom of God here on earth. She did such a good job seeing the holiness of God around her. I want to be more like her. Her beauty shone forth from her as she gave her life in the service of others. She was actually a queen, a legitimate royal. She knew what it was like to be the highest in the kingdom and to be waited on by servants. When she was eating dinner and asked for more dipping sauce, she got more dipping sauce. And fast!

But she didn't get caught up in that. She didn't cling to that treatment to make her feel good about herself, letting the attention go to her head and making her more bossy. Instead, because of her conversion to Christianity, she spent her days in the castle in service of the poor. She saw the holiness and the goodness of God in every poor, sick, and dying soul that she served. Elizabeth even gave up her fancy clothes and wore peasant's attire in order that the poor would trust her and see her as one of them, instead of as an unapproachable queen.

She built a hospital to care for the sick and dying and every day she dedicated time to go and hand out food to the poor in the town. Her spirituality drove her to not only find God in church and in the sacraments, but she found Him in the world around her. She participated in the Kingdom of God here and now and saw that the good material things she had in life were useless if she didn't use them to serve a higher purpose. She used all of her possessions and wealth to bless others. Her generosity brought life and goodness to those who encountered her.

That is what it means to live out the Good News of the Resurrection. It means seeing the potential holiness and goodness of the things some people would label as "worldly." Elizabeth knew that beauty wasn't only inside the walls of the church; all the rest of creation was humming with God's beauty, too. She was a queen but more importantly she was a member of the Kingdom of God.

As I strive to participate more and more in the redeemed world of the Kingdom of God, what God tells me is that, "You will seek me and find me when you seek me with all your heart" (Jeremiah 29:13). Those are some of the words that God has used to sing me back on track when all I see around me is ugliness and brokenness — especially when I look in the mirror.

If I'm not seeking the Divine, it can be tough to find God. If all I'm looking for when I look in the mirror are my flaws and imperfections — that is certainly all I will see. But if with all my heart I seek God, His grace will make up for what I lack and He will reveal Himself inside me. I am a part of the

Kingdom of God. I am royalty. I see that within my face in the mirror and I see that when He made me, He made me good. I see that I am beautiful when I love myself and others. I see I am beautiful when I enter into authentic connection with my friends. I see I am beautiful when I surrender my fears and insecurities to Him, like a child giving their broken things to their father to fix. I am beautiful when I am honest with myself and with God. I am beautiful because I am His and He made me so.

That's what I call being made new! I never thought I would get to that place in my heart back when I was trying to fill my life with attention and affirmation to make me feel "pretty." What I needed to learn was that everything around me hums with the sacred, and since I've been welcomed into God's family... so do I.

Practically Speaking:

My challenge for you is to seek out grace. We desperately need God's grace in order to see the Kingdom of God here and now. We need His grace to overcome our affinity and tendency to sin and break the cycle of distortion and disruption in our relationship with Him. So, when was the last time you went to Mass, Confession, or spent time in prayer one on one with God? Those are all sure ways of increasing His presence and His grace in your life. You have to put in the time and effort. I hear so many people complain that they feel like they have no relationship with God, but when I ask how their prayer life is, or how often they're seeking out the sacraments they say, "Well... not that much." And therein lies the problem. It's like any relationship. You have to show up and work at it. You will start to see God and His Divine ways all around you, including in your own soul... but, here's the catch... you have to seek God with your whole heart, not half of it.

GIVERS WILL RECEIVE

I've never sat amongst a more bizarre group of people than when I donated plasma. There were car mechanics, still covered in grease from the garage. There were men and women in business suits, still answering emails on their phones. There was a joyful, chatty middle-aged man sitting in a wheelchair because he had no legs. Young, college-aged girls loudly gossiping with the person sitting next to them. A handful of people who were most likely living on the streets. And then there was me. A girl with college debt looming over her like a storm cloud and a mailbox full of bills I wasn't sure how I would pay.

So twice a week, after my day-job, I spent about 2-3 hours waiting in line and lying on a medical recliner that still smelled like the last person because the staff didn't *quite* wipe the whole thing with a disinfectant wipe. I did it so often I knew all the people that worked there. I made just enough money to cover my bills. And in return I now have a permanent scar on the inside of my arm from where they would stick the needle into me.

I clearly did it for the money, but also a small (very small) part of me felt good about making a contribution to the sick people who needed that plasma to continue living. My literal "gift of self" was making a difference. I can't think about it too hard, though, because then I start imagining another person whose body is full of the liquid that was once in MY body, and ew.

Much more rewarding for me is to give of myself in ways where I can love the people around me. In college, I remember in one of the dorm bathrooms there was a sign with the quote: "Man cannot fully find himself, except through a sincere gift of himself." Saint John Paul II said that and the more often I used the bathroom (hence every day) the more I read that quote and it was imbedded deep in my heart and mind. It seems so contradictory when you first read it. The more of yourself you give away as a gift, the more you find out who you are? It was tough to wrap my mind around that so I kept turning it over in my mind and heart. I'm not one to just accept something just because a saint said it. Not everything they say is pure gold. They're saints because of their virtue, not because everything they wrote was profound and perfectly true. If I become a saint someday, you'll see — my journal entries and birthday cards to my mom are just as normal as everyone else's.

The more I pondered the quote and the more I put it to the test in my own life, the more I understood it to be true. I understood that this could be transformatory for my desire to discover my inner beauty.

The ultimate, final gift of Jesus was the gift of His whole self on the cross, right? Total self-gift. It was the most beautiful thing He did for us. (I say that despite the fact that Him multiplying endless loaves of bread is pretty high on the list. Because carbs.)

Here's how it works, in my understanding: God made me and when He made me, He made me a little tiny bit like Him (Genesis 1:27). He is a Trinity of three persons, Father, Son, and Holy Spirit. They exist in an endless cycle of love and self-gift of one to another. They exist in community. When I give what is all mine — my time, talents, thoughts, heart, (and plasma) — to another person out of charity and love, those parts of me only expand and grow. It doesn't take away anything that I have, I only get more — more grace, more love, more joy, more peace — and those are godly qualities. The more I give of myself, the more united I can be with God.

And (we've been over this before but...) remember what God is? He is beauty. So the more I give of myself in self-gift, the more I can experience God's beauty and be open to that beauty dwelling in me. My eyes can be opened to the beauty within me when I get rid of the selfishness and greed and pride that holds me back from making a gift of myself. Those things are like a fog keeping me from seeing the beauty of the garden of my soul. But when I serve others, when I deny my own wants in order to help someone else, that fog of selfishness is lifted a little, and I get a new little glimpse of my beauty. It's amazing!

One time, when I worked hard at making a gift of my time, talents, and my heart, I saw my beauty more clearly in the way my heart grew in patience and selflessness. It's a good story, too.

One Thanksgiving my mom and dad came to stay at my house for the holiday. I had never cooked a thanksgiving meal before so I was super excited to put my culinary skills to the test and make the best Thanksgiving they ever had. The best.

For weeks I picked out all the right recipes and ingredients and serving dishes. I was so excited. When Thanksgiving Day arrived, everything was going well. Dad and I had to run an errand and mom said she wanted to stay home and maybe take Riley, my dog, for a walk. Sounds nice right? Maybe if your mom isn't super petite and your dog isn't almost 100 lbs and sometimes a little nuts on a leash. So I said to her, "Okay, but be careful because if that dog sees a cat it will pull on the leash very hard because cats are food, not friends."

"Please don't lose my dog," were my parting words as I walked out the door.

I'm sure you have a hint where this is going. Dad and I got back from our errand, and walked in the house. My mom was sitting in the living room crying! My first thought was that the dog had run away. My second thought was, "At least I don't have to buy dog food anymore." I'm kidding! My second thought was, "Is my mom okay?!" Then Riley came prancing in to greet me, so I knew my first fear hadn't come to pass.

Through tears my mom told us what happened. The walk was going well for the first 98% of it. Then, sure enough, on their way home as they were not even 50 yards from my house, Riley spotted a cat. I can just imagine her eyes zeroing in on the cat for a second before she made a dash for it. One second the dog is nicely walking along, the next she's full-charge-ahead as fast as she can up the neighbor's driveway. Any slack that was in the leash was immediately pulled taut and with my words "please don't lose my dog" still ringing in her ears, my mother was determined to not let go of that leash. The dog was so strong and my mom so petite she couldn't stand her ground and yank the dog back into submission. Instead the dog yanked HER into submission and my mom fell face down on the ground and the dog dragged my mom's prostrate body up the whole driveway. Have you ever heard of a dog that strong and that motivated to attack a cat?

My mom said she was mainly shaken up, and a little sore from her fall but that she was okay. I was so glad nothing had "majorly" gone wrong because that would sure put a damper on this "perfect" Thanksgiving I was trying to host.

We moved on, got some frozen peas for my mom to use like an ice pack, and I started making dinner.

A couple hours later, I was ready to serve my epic and perfect Thanksgiving dinner. I called my parents to the table as I laid down the steaming platters of green beans, turkey, potatoes, and biscuits. My mom limped and hobbled over to the table, holding her sides and wincing in pain. We all prayed before the meal, thanking God for the glorious food I had prepared so perfectly. We started serving everything and my dad realized there was no gravy. How could I forget the gravy? Oh well, we decided to roll with it.

Except that about two bites into the meal, my mom gets up and dashes to the bathroom to throw up. She was in so much pain it was making her nauseous. My dad ran in there to check on her but soon came back because she said she just needed a moment to catch her breath.

Two *more* bites into dinner and my dad gets up and dashes to the bathroom to throw up! The turkey was so painfully dry, and so in desperately in need of gravy, that he had literally choked on it!

They both came out and said we needed to go the emergency room asap. Dad was just recovering from the turkey, but mom was not okay after the dog-dragged-me-up-the-driveway incident.

We left the food on the table and spent the next couple hours in the ER, which turned out to be a lot more fun for my mom because of the blessing of morphine. She had quite a bit of bruising and pain, nothing was broken and I was able to return them safely to their hotel that night.

I went back to my house to see the cold thanksgiving dinner still sitting where we left it on the table. My gravy-less dinner that was supposed to help facilitate a picture perfect family memory had failed. For a moment, I felt like my gift was one more thing that wasn't good enough. I had tried to do something loving and selfless but... did it work? Can you really count a holiday you host as a win when your guests end up vomiting and in the emergency room?

I served myself a plate of green beans and stuck them in the microwave, then sat on the couch to eat them alone because a sad, pathetic pity party was what I deserved.

Or was it?

When Jesus went to a dinner party, He didn't make it all about the food. It was about the heart of the host.

Jesus was walking through a town one day and there was a crowd and a lot of commotion that accompanied Him. This guy named Zacchaeus wanted to see what the fuss was all about. However, he was vertically challenged (aka short like a troll) so he climbed a tree to get a better view. When Jesus got to the tree where Zacchaeus was, He looked up and saw him there. When I imagine this story, I bet Jesus was amused at this point. I bet He was also encouraged to know that people were interested and that they had some curiosity and maybe some hope that He was the Messiah.

Jesus says his name, just like He calls Mary Magdalene by name in the garden. He says, "Zacchaeus, come down immediately, I must stay at your house today." I'm pretty sure if I was Zacchaeus and Jesus first of all knows my name and calls it out among the crowd, and second of all invites Himself over — I would NOT be able to say no either!

It was an invitation from Jesus inviting Zacchaeus to be a gift-giver, to offer the self-gift that is hospitality. This was a huge deal, too, because Zacchaeus wasn't the kind of person who was applauded in the society he lived in, so he was the last person that people expected Jesus to chill with. He was a tax collector of high rank, which essentially meant he was a professional at ripping people off. He was well-off, but not because he had worked hard and worked honestly. I mean (sorry, Zacchaeus, to put it this way)... he was kind of a crook.

And that no-good-dirty-rotten-crook with his dishonest-dirty-rotten-stolen-money was the one who Jesus wanted to hang out with that evening. Because that's who Jesus is, the Shepherd who goes the extra mile to seek out His lost sheep, the one who had fallen into a life of sin and was separating himself from God's grace.

Zacchaeus took one small step toward God by climbing up the tree to simply look at Jesus, and God did the rest. Jesus entered into Zacchaeus' mess and sat there with him, talked with him, listened to him, shared a meal and fellowship with him. Jesus allowed Zacchaeus to give the gift of himself, however much or little he had to give. And it made all the difference for Zacchaeus' life. He made a public proclamation of conversion and repentance! He told Jesus he wanted to change his ways and, to make reparation for the wrong done to all those he had cheated, he would pay them back four times the amount he had taken. What a day for that town! You get a refund! And you get a refund! And YOU get a refund!

I love how that quote from St. John Paul II is illustrated here. "Man cannot fully find himself, except through a sincere gift of himself." Zacchaeus had this moment of self-awareness where he looked at his life and sins squarely and said, "Not this anymore," to them. That moment came because he made a gift of himself and his time and his home and his food to God. He sat and began a relationship with God. He was honest, maybe for the first time in a long time. It wasn't all about the meal; it was about his heart. That's what self-gift is, it's sharing who we honestly are with the person in front of us even though we may not have it all together and even though we only have our sinful selves to offer.

When I made that Thanksgiving meal for my parents, and then felt bad about it and dejected, it was because I was putting the emphasis on the meal instead of the honest, authentic gift of myself — and that had been there too! I really had been present. We sat in that emergency room talking and laughing and taking selfies to remember "The Thanksgiving Debacle of 2013."

As I went to bed that night after looking back on the day, I realized my heart did feel more full. I felt (dare I say it) beautiful. Because I had spent my day not just cooking a meal and sitting in the hospital, but I spent my day being loving, patient, self-less, and caring. And those virtues replaced in me a little bit of the pride, and impatience, and selfishness, and indifference that also festers in my heart. I was a tiny bit closer to God. And that is beauty I could feel within me, not that I saw in my reflection in the mirror.

I think that the saints who are able to make really grand gestures of self-gift, the ones we read about in saint-books centuries later had to start out by making tiny gifts of self in their day to day life.

Like St. Gianna Molla, for example. She gave the ultimate gift of her whole life for the sake of her child! But you don't wake up one day ready to give your life for someone else. This woman lived her whole life giving of herself to others, emptying her soul of it's attachments to self-interest and pride.

Gianna was born in the 1920's, meaning she's another saint who lived so recently that we have great photographs of her. She was a pediatrician and it sounds like she was the kind of doctor everyone wants. She really listened and cared for each of her patients personally. She loved having a direct connection to mothers and their children so that she could talk to them about the beauty of family life and what a gift each child is from God. Doctor Gianna treated each of her patients as if they were Jesus she was welcoming into her presence, just like Zacchaeus welcomed Jesus into his home. Because Jesus said that when you care for others, you care for Him, Gianna believed passionately in the importance of her work as a Catholic doctor. She wrote, "The day will come when we will become aware of others around us, and when this happens we will become new persons."

Gianna is saying that in being aware of others versus only thinking about ourselves, we turn over a new chapter of our lives. When we strive to not only think of me, myself, and I, but instead think of others, that virtue of selflessness that grows makes us new people. We find ourselves when we forget ourselves. We are more beautiful the more we serve others.

This is the principle she lived as a wife and mother too. Though she felt a strong pull to be a missionary, after much soul-searching and prayer, Gianna realized she was called to be a wife a mother. She met a wonderful Catholic man and they had three children together, while she also continued working as a pediatrician.

Gianna spent so much time caring for others — her patients, her children, loving her husband, and caring for the poor. She juggled family life and her medical career like the lady boss she was. It's amazing. Even when things got stressful at home and her husband needed a long vacation by himself, she held down the fort through the struggle. Her life was a gift to others, and the benefit she reaped was that she only gained more joy, more peace, and more union with God. Gianna became more of herself -- a better, more holy, more beautiful version of herself.

When she was pregnant with her fourth child, she developed some complications on top of what was already a difficult pregnancy. She had a tumor on her uterus and though it wasn't cancerous, it still needed to be removed for fear it would grow bigger and cause abnormalities in her new child. As soon as she found out about this, without hesitation she chose the surgery that was the least harmful to her child. She said, "If you must decide between me and the child, do not hesitate: choose the child — I insist on it. Save the baby."

Can you imagine? She had a full and wonderful life, but she didn't have it in her to do anything but make herself, including her body and potentially her whole life, to her unborn child.

The surgery went alright, but when it came time for her to give birth, she had a rough labor. The doctors opted to delivery the baby by C-section, probably making that choice because of the previous trauma her body had been under because of the surgery to remove the tumor.

Right after the C-section she developed an infection and within a week she died. Gianna was able to hold her new daughter for such a short time. She suffered immensely in the last couple days of her life, so much so that her husband likened it to the slow, painful sacrifice of Christ on the cross.

Could I handle a cross like that? St. Gianna's story sits in my heart and burns with that question. Am I strong enough to give my life for another? That sacrifice requires a strength of character that when I'm blunt and honest with myself, I'm scared I don't have.

Can I be that beautiful?

What I've come to understand about it is that God, in His wisdom, asks of us what He knows we're ready for. Before Gianna gave the self-gift of her whole life, first God asked her to give up her time and spend years studying to become a doctor. I bet there were a lot of days when it was so difficult to sit through one more lecture or shadow one more doctor.

And then God asked her to give of herself in loving her husband. And I don't know how much you know about dudes, but sometimes they can be a pain to love. As wonderful as men are, sometimes they're a little messy, or a little loud, or in Gianna's case, her husband needed alone time, which was really difficult for her to deal with.

Little by little God asked her to love others, and little by little she grew closer to Him and His beauty, more and more herself as she was more and more in union with Him.

God isn't asking me right now to give my life. He's asking me to make a self-gift by loving the people around me. He wants me to love the cashier at the grocery store who wants to chat with me when I don't feel like talking and the friend who needs someone to go to the mall with because they hate shopping for dresses and need encouragement. God asks you to do the dishes when there are no forks left for anyone to use and your brother is trying to stab his plate of chicken with a spoon. Selflessness is spending an extra 30 minutes at night baking store-bought cookie dough for your friend's birthday when you would rather be sleeping.

What I've realized is that those are the small, everyday, ordinary things that are transforming me into a "new person" as St. Gianna said. I don't feel it in the day to day, but when I look back over the years I think I can see it happening. Today, I know I am beautiful when I serve others. But years ago when I was only focused on how "pretty" I was or was not, I allowed myself to be so consumed by that thought that I didn't even have the motivation to go out and serve others. I only saw myself and in only looking at my flaws I was holding myself back from becoming more fully me.

What an incredible paradox. In giving we receive. From self-gift I become a more beautiful version of myself.

Even if that self-gift is just a plasma donation. Or a failed turkey dinner.

Practically Speaking:

Self-gift is pretty easy to put into practice because we live in a needy, needy world. If you're not seeing opportunities to practice giving of yourself — your time, talents, money, skills — then you're eyes aren't open wide enough!

The first people God has given us to love and serve are the people we are closest to in our homes, schools, jobs, and communities. It's like St. Teresa of Calcutta said, "What can you do to promote world peace? Go home and love your family."

Start with brainstorming ways you can love those people who are closest to you. In the beginning of your day ask God to bless your day and give Him permission to allow you to encounter those whom He wants you to serve. Like Zacchaeus climbing the tree, we have to make the first effort and then God will take it from there.

To jump start your brainstorming, here are some things that I have done: babysit for free for a mom who needs help, cook a meal (even if it's mac and cheese) for your friends and/or family, write cards to people just because, smile at everyone you walk by, buy coffee for the person behind you in line at a coffee shop, be vulnerable with your close friends and talk about what's really going on in your heart so that they know they're not alone in their struggles.

A BEAUTIFUL IMPERFECTION

I don't have it all figured out. As I said when I first started writing this book, I'm still working on all these principles. I think that writing has heightened my awareness of how much I still need to grow in my ability to listen to and live by God's words of truth. Not only that, but I also need to live by the example of so many women who came before us and left us an example of what true beauty is.

The last lesson that I want to leave you with is this — you may never feel like you've perfectly mastered all these lessons. And that is okay. If I've learned anything it's that we can never be perfect, and the more I reflect on it, I don't think I want to be. I have found that I see my beauty in my imperfection because it is in imperfection that we see more clearly our goals, it sharpens the vision of where we are and where we want to go. Imperfection gives us the chance to experience God's perfect love and gentle mercy. If I didn't struggle with these things, I wouldn't have a heightened awareness to listen for His voice singing me back on track when I get off the beat. If I was perfectly aware at all times of how God has infused His own beauty into my being, I wouldn't need the solace of prayer, or the connection and community and inspiration I find among the women saints.

Imperfection is beautiful because "imperfect" allows God to fill in what we are lacking.

God doesn't expect us to be perfect in the ways that the world does; He made us to be good and open to His grace. Remember, in Genesis He said, "It is good!"

The good things in life are the things that make us feel deep in our souls an amazement and a joy we can't quite articulate. It's the things we don't have words for because words don't do it justice. So then we use phrases and images that kind of get close but at the same time don't even scratch the surface.

It's so good to finish running a race. One time I ran a half marathon except I didn't run it as much as I slow-jogged it. And then around mile seven something happened to my leg and I was in incredible pain so I jogged/walked/limped the last six miles. It was brutal. At mile ten, I cried. At mile 11, I sobbed. At mile 12, I thought I couldn't possibly go on. And then I crossed the finish line. It was over and it was so, so good! There was sweat, tears, and blood from the blisters on my feet but oh man was it a good feeling. It wasn't perfect. Far from it. But it was good. And it was good precisely because it was imperfect. The difficulties and pain made the glory of the finish line so much better!

Imagine having a friend who is perfect in every way. They always know exactly the perfect gift to give you or they always have the perfect words to say. They never mess up. Everything about them is perfect. Besides you thinking they may be an artificially intelligent robot, you would also probably think the relationship was boring. Part of the goodness of friendship is the imperfection of it. It's the laughter that ensues because you couldn't find a perfect gift so you got them ridiculous socks that won't even fit their large feet. It's the fact that on Monday you cry to them about your disaster of a life, and then on Tuesday they feel comfortable enough to cry to you about how they are a hot mess, too. That builds a beautiful friendship because it is good... not perfect. And it's the imperfections that make it good.

I've saved my favorite gospel story for last. This is one that Jesus told when He was "accused" of letting the less-than-perfect people hang out and eat with Him. The "scribes and Pharisees," who saw themselves as a higher class and more perfect than others, started complaining about these imperfect people who were allowed to be with Jesus.

Jesus' rebuttal is the story of *The Prodigal Son*. If you're not familiar with it, the story goes like this: A father has two sons, one is a goody-goody who always does what he's told and thinks that his good actions are what make him good — his worth is built upon his actions. The second son is all — "I WANT TO PARTY. CAN'T STOP. WON'T STOP." So he asks his father for the money he will get when his father dies (which is essentially like saying, "Hey Dad, I wish you were already dead"). He takes the money, parties like a freshman in college, then realizes he's so poor he doesn't even have money for food. Not even a gas station hot dog (or whatever the equivalent would be in Jesus' time). The son realizes he should drag his sorry butt home and try to see if he can work for his dad. He figures his father would never be cool with welcoming him back and treating him like he used to be treated. Now that they had had the whole "I wish you were dead, can I have that money" talk — things could never be the same.

Or so he thought.

This is where it gets good. Party boy heads home. Dad is watching and waiting for him to come home, sees him from a distance, and runs out to meet him! Party boy is very confused. Dad says there's no way he'll let him work as a servant, he's a beloved child! They throw party boy a party because that's what he loves (duh). Older son is not pleased. So the father tries to talk him into joining the party to which the guy turns up his nose saying he is the one that should be celebrated because he's always done things perfectly for the father. And then the father drops this line: "'Son, you are always with me, and all that is mine is yours" (Luke 15:31).

It was never about being perfect because God made us good and that is enough. The lesson I believe Jesus is teaching the scribes and Pharisees is that the spiritual life is not about earning God's favor through doing things the perfect way. He loves us as His children regardless of what we do and/or don't accomplish. His love is unchanging. He has the fullness of life for us. Those words, "Everything I have is yours," are so beautiful and hopeful to me. Imagine God saying those words to you, "My daughter... everything I have is yours."

No matter how much the younger son messed up, he was still loved the same. No matter how poorly or how well the older son obeyed his father and did everything "right," he was loved just the same.

Can you just imagine Jesus telling this story and how angry the scribes and Pharisees must have been when He finished? Here they were thinking that what made them great in the eyes of God were all the things they were doing perfectly, and all the laws that they were upholding perfectly. And here is Jesus saying that those sinners sitting around us, those people who can't manage to fulfill all the Jewish laws all the time... they are loved just the same. They may not be perfect, but they are good... oh so good in the eyes of our Heavenly Father.

The father in the story of *The Prodigal Son* has no judgment, no harsh words, no scornful look on his face as the party-boy-son comes home. He has an embrace for him. Nothing changes his love. His children are always beautiful in his eyes, no matter their flaws and imperfections.

I can't help but marvel at how this story from the Bible is so much like the story of St. Margaret of Cortona. Oh my gosh, talk about an inspiring woman.

She was this rich dude's mistress. Actually, even before she was this guy's mistress everyone knew her as super scandalous, always having men around her, and generally leading a life of deplorable sin. Margaret was this way probably because she loved attention and affection and wasn't getting it at home. The men in her town saw her as a pretty face and made her feel validated and loved. Which, at our core, is what we all want and need, right? We want to feel valuable and beautiful. We want to be someone's beloved because that means they see and appreciate our beauty — who we are as a person.

Margaret eventually left the town she grew up in and found a job as a servant in the castle of a nobleman. The nobleman took a liking to her, recognizing how pretty she was, just like all the men did. He fell in love with her but couldn't make her his wife since he was of a higher class. She became his mistress and was there for him sexually, but wasn't given the status or honor of being his wife. They had a child together.

Margaret was living in the castle, caring for their newborn, expected to be available to this man whenever he wanted sex, and struggling with feeling really alone. She had discovered through trial and error that this life of sin she had chosen, which was so different from her Catholic upbringing, wasn't leading her to fulfillment and joy and an abundant life. Margaret was only seen as a pretty face, not appreciated for the beautiful woman God had made her to be.

During this time, as she was struggling with loneliness, she also spent a lot of time thinking about God and her soul. I imagine her feeling like she could never take back all that she had done and what her life had become. How could God ever take her back? She was far from what I'm sure was applauded as the "perfect, Catholic girl" — she was less like St. Clare who had just founded the Poor Clare order of nuns... and more like Mary Magdalene, pre-Jesus encounter and conversion. The culture that Margaret was surrounded by was prone to emphasizing how big, bad, and evil sin is. There was even this group of super-religious-fanatics who would parade through the streets whipping themselves to atone for any sin they had committed! Talk about intense!

I bet Margaret felt like she was stuck... that even if she wanted to escape her life of sin it would be impossible. How could she care for the child on her own? Wouldn't the child's father be upset and come after them if she tried to leave? He was very attached to Margaret, after all. And who would take her in? Would her father welcome her back into his home? Would her Heavenly Father welcome her back into His arms? I bet her thoughts sounded a lot like that younger son in the story Jesus told.

Soon after their son was born, Margaret found the nobleman dead in the woods! As she looked down at his body on the ground, she couldn't help but wonder what had happened to his soul? That thought shook her down to her core and it was a turning point for her. She went back to the castle, grabbed the baby, and ran away from that town.

Something had clicked within her and she knew she had to do something drastic to turn her life around. So she did. She took matters into her own hands and began doing acts of penance (but none of that crazy "walking through the streets whipping yourself" stuff).

Some holy friars helped Margaret find good work and a safe home. She turned her life around, even though it was difficult. She still faced temptation, especially to sins of impurity, all the time. She kept turning her life over to God and through every temptation and every trial and every snide remark from people who only knew her as the crazy sinner, she grew in virtue. Her prayer life became extraordinary and through the guidance of her Confessor, she had a very personal and intimate relationship with God (which was later all written down by her Confessor).

As Margaret was dying, she had a vision of Mary Magdalene in heaven. I think it's safe to assume she felt a lot like Mary Magdalene, leading a life of sin before an encounter with God changed her life. Seeing Mary Magdalene in heaven was probably a huge consolation for her. It was as if God was showing her a little glimpse into the glory that would be in her near future too — the transformation that is possible from sinner to saint. Jesus told Margaret that when He speaks of Mary Magdalene He says, "This is my beloved daughter" just as God had opened the heavens and said about Jesus, "This is my beloved Son" at His baptism in the River Jordan.

"My beloved daughter"... those words seem like an emotional embrace from God. Those are the words that Margaret heard from the lips of Jesus to let her know how He sees us. He doesn't see the sin and brokenness; He doesn't count how many times we've fallen.

God is a Father like in the story of *The Prodigal Son* who is watching and waiting for us to return home to His arms. He only sees the one He loves — and that is you, in all your imperfections.

God wants us no matter what. You are His beloved daughter no matter what. No matter how well you can see and rejoice in your inner beauty, He still loves you. Even if you try 99 times to look in the mirror and see more than a pretty face, but only one time do you succeed, He still loves you.

He loves you when you hate on yourself. He loves you even though you say mean things to yourself. He loves you despite the way you try to find love in other ways, like the ways you search for validation, grasping at the littlest bits from guys or attention on social media. He loves you when you feel like a nobody or when you feel important and recognized.

God knows that deep down we just want to be loved. We want to be someone's beloved. So, to that deepest need of our hearts He whispers, "You are my beloved daughter." That is the main chorus of the song He is singing over your heart. You are beautiful because you are His.

Everything else that we fixate on as our flaws and our imperfections — they never mattered to God anyway. Those things have never defined us, nor will they ever define us. There are a hundred ways a day that I fail to see my beauty, or love myself unconditionally, or make decisions based on a simple childlike trust and surrender to my Father. I mess up. Still to this day, I don't always look in the mirror and see a beautiful woman — but I have improved so immensely and I'll keep trying. I've come so far, but when I fall back into any old patterns, when I start listening to that broken record of lies again and lose the beat of God's song, I go back to prayer, I go back to those quiet moments when I can connect with my Savior and I ask Him to sing me back on track all over again. I say, "Tell it to me again. Refresh my memory; renew my heart in Your love. I need to see myself through Your eyes. I need You to tell me again how I am Your beloved daughter." And the more I ask, the more I search with my whole heart, the easier it becomes to hear the voice of my Shepherd leading me back to the beat of His heart. That beat which is just for me because I am His beloved daughter.

Then I see my beauty. I look in the mirror and I see a glimpse of God because I see an immortal soul with His beauty inscribed into the cells and the fibers of my being.

And I know without a doubt once again that I am good. I am His. I am more than a pretty face. I am beautiful.

Practically Speaking:

One of the practical things I've done that helped me to let go of the perfectionism rooted deep in my heart telling me I was never perfect enough was writing letters to myself at different points in time letting myself off the hook for things. It's like a letter forgiving yourself for all your flaws. I knew I needed to accept the fact that I am not perfect, that I am a person who fails and I always will, so I wrote a letter to myself listing my flaws and failures and then talked about how it's okay.

Try it. Write yourself a letter of forgiveness. First, invite God into the process, start with a prayer that He'll help you forgive yourself for being imperfect. Thank yourself for trying so hard to be perfect, but let yourself know that you are good. It may feel funny talking to yourself in third person. However, it's nice to force yourself to take a bird's eye view of your day to day life in order to point out the good and the bad and say, "I see you're trying your best, let's allow that to be good enough without setting an unrealistic standard of perfection." Tell yourself of God's love for you despite whatever your struggles, sins, and imperfections are. Once you're done, read it over and try to believe it. You can keep repeating this exercise as often as necessary, or read over the one letter again and again.

LIFE TEEN

Leading Teens Closer to Christ
www.LifeTeen.com